Karma Philosophy

Virchand Raghavji Gandhi

Born on 25th August 1864 in Mahuva, Gujarat

Died on 7th August 1901 at Mahuwar near Mumbai

Karma Philosophy

Speeches and Writings of

Virchand Raghavji Gandhi

The Jain Delegate to the Parliament of Religions; Chicago, U.S.A.

Compiled and Edited by

Bhagu F. Karbhari

Kaveri Books
New Delhi – 110 002

Karma Philosophy: Speeches and Writings of Virchand Raghavji Gandhi; The Jain Delegate to the Parliament of Religions; Chicago, U.S.A.

Compiled and Edited by: Bhagu F. Karbhari

First Published in 1913
Edition 2022

ISBN: 978-81-955493-7-5

Published by
Kaveri Books
4832/24, Ansari Road, Darya Ganj
New Delhi-110002 (India)
Tel.: 011-2328 8140, 4707 2321
E-mail: kaveribooks@gmail.com
Web: www.kaveribooks.com

PRINTED IN INDIA

श्री महावीराय नमः
श्रीमत् सुदर्शन गुरवे नमः

A Tribute in Memory of
Great Jain Saint of North India

Sangh Shasta Shashan Prabhavak
Gurudev Shri Sudarshan Lal Ji Maharaj

who inspired and illuminated light
in the lives of millions of people to follow
the righteous path of non-violence and truth

— Guru Parivar

Gurudev Shri Sudarshan Lal Ji Maharaj:
A Tribute

A great soul and a great saint of Jain religion in Northern India, Gurudev Shri Sudarshan Lal ji Maharaj was born on 04 April 1923 to an advocate Shri Chandagi Ram ji in Rohtak, a city in Haryana. His mother was Smt. Sundari Devi, a religious lady who left heavenly abode in his childhood. His grandfather, popularly known as Baba Jaggumal ji Maharaj, took *diksha* in the year of 1937 at the ripe age of 52 under the pious feet of Vyakhyan Vachapsati Gurudev Shri Madan Lal ji Maharaj, one of the most renowned saint in those times. Gurudev Shri Sudarshan Lal ji Maharaj was greatly inspired by his grandfather, followed his footsteps and took *diksha* on 18th January, 1942 in the pious feet of Vyakhyan Vachapsati Shri Madan Lal ji Maharaj. After attaining sainthood in the initial years, Gurudev spent his entire time looking after his gurus and in study of scriptures. He studied different languages like Sanskrit, Hindi, Punjabi, Urdu, Prakrit, Farsi, Gujarati and English and possessed good command over these. He traveled extensively bare footed and spread his spiritual holiness in the regions of Punjab, Haryana, Jammu, Himachal, Rajasthan, Uttar Pradesh and Delhi. Twenty-nine disciples under his mentorship joined him in his journey of preaching about living a pious life to millions of people. People worshipped him like a God in his life time and still do. After spreading the message of spirituality for over five decades, he left for his heavenly abode on April 25, 1999 in New Delhi. But the message and the path shown by him will always illuminate light in the lives of millions of people.

— Guru Parivar

Virchand Raghavji Gandhi:
A Brief Note

The Buffalo Courier, an American newspaper, reported, "*Of all Eastern scholars, it was this young man whose lectures on Jainism and practices were listened to with the greatest interest and attention.*" But which youth was the Buffalo Courier talking about? He was none other than Virchand Raghavji Gandhi, a contemporary of Swami Vivekananda and Mahatma Gandhi, who represented Jainism at the World's first Parliament of Religions in Chicago in 1893. A forgotten Indian Jain scholar, aged just 29, addressed over 3000 delegates in the religious Parliament and enthralled the audience.

Virachand Raghavji Gandhi, a great soul, was born on 25 August 1864 to a businessman Raghavji Tejpalji Gandhi in Mahuva, a small town, near Bhavnagar in Gujrat. His father was a wealthy gentleman of the town but he was known for his honesty, integrity and religious inclination.

At an early age, Virchand attended a city school in Bhavnagar for his primary education. He was a dedicated student who excelled in the matriculation examination of Bombay University in the year 1880. He was a scholar with a voracious appetite for knowledge. He went to Bombay's Elphinstone College for higher education and obtained a bachelor's degree in law in 1884. During the same time, Virchand met Mahatma Gandhi, who later mentioned him in his autobiography, saying:

> "While in Bombay, I began, on one hand, my study of Indian law and, on the other, my experiments in

At the World Parliament of Religions:
L-R: Virchand Gandhi, Hewivitarne Dharmapala, Swami Vivekananda, and (possibly) G. Bonet Maury

> dietetics in which Virchand Gandhi, a friend, joined me. My brother, for his part, was trying his best to get me briefs. The study of Indian law was a tedious business... Virchand Gandhi was reading for the Solicitor's Examination and would tell me all sorts of stories about Barristers and Vakils."

For almost a decade, Virchand gave his lectures in more than fourteen languages, including Gujarati, Hindi, Bengali, English, Prakrit, Sanskrit and French. There is no doubt that he was a man of great potential and exceptional skill set. Therefore, it was not a mere coincidence, but he was destined to be at the Conference of world religions. He got a worthy opportunity when the organizers of the Parliament of Religions originally invited Acharya Vijay Anandasuri, popularly known as Muni Shri Atmaramji, a Jain monk and leading reformer, to speak at the Conference. A Jain monk's ideals of right conduct forbade him for travelling to America, which he could not do without a steamer as Jain monks could travel only on foot. But Muni Shri Atmaramji Maharaj wanted Jainism to be represented in the Congress. Therefore, he wrote a letter to the Jain Association of India in Bombay, requesting that someone be sent to the Congress to represent Jainism, and it was he who recommended Virchand Gandhi as an ambassador. Muni Shri believed in Virchand's abilities as the spokesman of the Jain religion and trained him for six months in the principles, practices and philosophy of Jainism.

Virchand then moved to America and represented Jainism, the only religion of absolute non-violence and peace, at the World Conference of Religions. He not only shared the stage with the great Swami Vivekananda who represented Hinduism, but also enthralled the audience with his lectures on Jainism.

The Congress of World Religions was a unique attempt to provide a forum for inter-religious dialogues for leaders of world religions. From all over the world, some wise, pious and curious, learned and eager religious leaders gathered at the Conference to express and present the tenets of their religions and to learn from others. The Congress held in Chicago provided a great opportunity for the comparative study of different religions. It was noble and unique in its concept, representation and sincerity of purpose.

Virchand Gandhi speeches left a deep and lasting impression on the minds of the American people. An eminent contemporary American wrote very eloquently about him at that time. He said that;

> "A number of distinguished Hindu scholars, philosophers and religious teachers attended and addressed the Parliament; some of them taking rank with the highest of any race for learning, eloquence and piety. But it is safe to say that no one of the oriental scholars was listened to with greater interest than was this young layman of the Jainas as he declared the Ethics and Philosophy of his people."

He discussed the age-old esoteric questions that baffled entire delegations of intellectuals. From the creation of the universe to its creator, from the presence of God to the ultimate purpose of life, Virchand covered all such topics. His speeches were so influential that he was later invited to lecture and address audiences in Boston, New York and Washington DC in the US and in European countries such as England, France and Germany. His knowledge was not limited to Jain philosophy and he spoke and wrote on a wide range of subjects ranging from the ancient Indian civilizations to the Indian international trading system, the science of food and the science of occult.

"In our country religion is not different from philosophy, and religion and philosophy do not differ from science." This quotation given by Virchand Gandhi proved that he was not only a Jain philosopher but he was also a true patriot. Virchand Gandhi was undoubtedly a brilliant scholar of Jainism who made the Jain philosophy of non-violence so simple that he received deep respect from the audience. As a result, he got his speeches published in full in many publications.

Beyond Jainism, Buddhism and Vedanta philosophy, he delivered hundreds of lectures on various other topics such as Yoga, Indian Philosophy, Indian Culture, Occultism and Spiritualism. He had acquired knowledge of Christianity and Western Philosophy. He had made a comparative study of different philosophies which instilled in him the confidence to discuss various subjects.

Virchand was a political activist also. He actively participated in India's movement for independence and represented the Bombay province at the Indian National Congress session in Pune 1895. His loyal associates like Justice Ranade and Premchand Roychand were very close to him.

The Gandhi Philosophical Society, The School of Oriental Philosophy, and The Society for the Education of Women of India were all created by Virchand Gandhi in America. He was a great supporter of women's rights as well as the ethical treatment of animals. He established the Jain Literature Society in England and taught Jainism there.

In 1901 in London, Virchand's health unexpectedly deteriorated and physicians advised him to return home. But he was firm on taking the examination for his degree in honours and in the month of June 1901 he cleared it and returned to India. After a month, on 07 August 1901, at the age of 37, Virchand died of pulmonary haemorrhage, in Mahuwar near Mumbai.

Deepak Rohilla

Author of *Say No To Spirituality*

Preface

I did not expect at the time when I first thought of bringing out the speeches and writings of the Late Mr. V. R. Gandhi, that they would furnish material for as many as more than three volumes. These were supplied to me by Mr. Umarosing Tank of Delhi, the late Mr. Virchand Dipchand, and Mr. Maneklal Ghelabhai of Bombay; for which I am deeply thankful to them. As a result the first volume entitled "The Jain Philosophy" was published in the year 1911. After its publication, the trustees of the Seth Devchand Lalbhai Jain Pustakoddhar Fund were pleased to include "Yoga Philosophy", the embodiment of the rest of my collected materials, in their series, which was published by them. These two publications were welcomed by Western scholars and readers, who took interest in the Jain theology and literature, which was a matter of great satisfaction to me. When "Yoga Philosophy" was published, I was in the dark if there were any further speeches and writings of Mr. Gandhi. However the materials embodied in this volume were supplied by Mr. H Warren of London, which are on the Karma Philosophy.

The Jains of all shades of opinion believe in the Law of Karma, to which every soul that is not yet emancipated, is subject. What that Law is and how by it the soul, or spirit is governed is explained in brief in the following pages. In the absence of an exhaustive work specially dealing with Karma, as it is understood by the Jains, this volume would be of immense use to the students of Jainism. No vivid and real idea of Jainism can be formed without a thorough conception of the law of karma.

In my preface to the Yoga Philosophy I have alluded to the deficiency of literature on Jainism in Western languages. This is however no less true of Indian Vernaculars in general. Would that those, whose duty it is to secure the permanence or the faith, awaken to this necessity. The times and circumstances are altered and the activities of the followers of the faith should also be adjusted, at least *proportionately*, in conformity with the needs of the situation. There should come into existence a class of Jain scholars and translators, who may well carry out this object. This however will continue to remain only a pious wish until the method of charities is relatively changed.

Bhagu F. Karbhari

Editor, The Jain, Bombay

Introduction

Jain literature, comprising as it does almost all the branches that are characteristic of ancient Indian literature, holds no insignificant niche in the gallery of that literature. It is considerable even as it is at present, and was more so in former times. This is not the proper place to enumerate the great writers and their works that constitute the glory of that literature. The fact that the Jain writers had flourished in great abundance in times gone by, is evident from the vast stock of literature that has survived to this day, though it is yet in an unexplored state. Their eminence in subject matter as well as language is manifest to those who are conversant with it.

Along with Indian literature at large, Jain literature too has been a participator in the unhappy fate it met with at the hands partly of alien bigotry, and partly of mutual religious jealousy and from the peculiarities of the climate. There was a time when there was no other alternative to secure the very existence of such literature but that of burying it in subterranean archives. The very method employed for the safety of the works became later on instrumental in further diminishing the stock and that at a time when there was not the least chance of its being further enriched. Those upon whom had fallen the task of being the hereditary custodians of such collections, had inherited the traditions of their forefathers, *viz.*, those of not suffering any part of such collection to see the rays of the Sun, lest they might be deprived of them, and the works most dear to them be destroyed by the assailants. It is very strange indeed that these traditions are alive even at this day when there is peace all round, and when the time is most propitious for the development of literature. Fire even has contributed its quota to the destruction of the records. Add to these the all round degeneration among the followers of the faith, when far from the prospects of further expansion, the faith was in imminent danger of being extinct. It was during this time that more attention was paid to the performance of external rites and ceremonies, and practically nothing was done in the direction of education and literature and the stirring up of the inner spirit of faith. It is only very recently that a practical revival of a salutary character is visible. Owing to circumstances above mentioned, the literary results of the arduous labour and the great learning of the Acharyas and the Sadhus of the faith, could not be made accessible.

In conclusion we have to say that this volume contains the speeches and writings of the late Mr. Virchand R. Gandhi. We have nothing to add here about this work, as enough has been said about it in the preface written by Mr. B. F. Karbhari. We are thankful to him for having supplied us with the materials for this publication.

Naginbhai Ghelabhai Javeri

Contents

KARMA

OR

The Law of Moral Causation

There are one or two principles which must be mentioned upon which the doctrine of karma is based, in order that it may be understood: first, that this universe is not a mere congeries of substances set together and set into motion by some authority, but is a system of itself, subject to laws inherent in its own constitution. And such law is a proposition derived from our observation of the universe, which proposition teaches us that certain phenomena occur regularly in certain circumstances. The law is, therefore, not a command, but a formula.

Second, that the phenomenon of life, and also of consciousness, is different, not only in degree, but in kind, from the phenomenon known as activity of matter (motion, or vibration). In the activity of matter there is growth by addition in dead objects, subject only to chemical laws. Whereas the living being takes to itself particles foreign to those that are in the body and changes their nature, and assimilates them with its own body, suspending when necessary chemical action; and in living beings there is the reproduction of the species. These characteristics are not possessed by dead objects. With reference to consciousness, the difference is more marked. Consciousness can never be identical with motion; they may go together, and one may even be dependent upon the other; but they are different. Consciousness is a synthesis, and not a motion. It is a synthesis of perceptions and conceptions. Consciousness and life have some substance other than material substance; but still it is real substance. It is a substance which is not cognized by the senses, but objects which can be known by the senses do not exhaust the whole universe. The substratum (so to speak) of life and consciousness is the 'soul' or 'atman'. Consciousness is an experience; the consciousness of one person cannot be the consciousness of another. You may *know* another man's consciousness but you cannot *have* another man's consciousness. Hence each person's individuality is entirely different from the individuality of another: one 'atman' does not become another 'atman.'

So there are these principles – (i) the universe is a system, and (ii) there are 'atmans' or souls which can have no beginning or end: you cannot postulate a beginning to a reality.

A reality in order to be real need not be changeless. A reality should pass through varying changes and states. To be, to exist, according to the Jain philosophy, would mean to stand in relation to something else, to be the cause of, to be influenced by, and to influence. Hence, because the soul is a reality (or the individual is a reality) it must have passed in the past through many conditions and states, and because it is a reality it would not entirely disappear at death but will exist and continue to exist in some state or other at all times. Every stage of existence is the result of the previous state.

Definition of Karma

The doctrine which gives us some explanation as to how certain characteristics or factors of our individuality which we have at present – how these factors were produced as a resultant of forces generated in the past, this doctrine is the doctrine of karma.

Karma is according to the Jain philosophy a reality, as real as the walls around us are, only the walls we see, but the karma one cannot see. There is not only *one* reality called karma, because karma with each person is different. Karma is that finest matter which a living being attracts to itself by reason of certain impellent forces which are in the individual; not only attracted to but assimilated by the individual itself (this doctrine of karma applies not only to human, but to all living beings); and it changes the individuality of the living being. It has become a kind of stored force, and just as a compressed spring of a watch will expand at some time, so the stored force of karma will manifest itself at some time or other. Hence it produces some kind of experience at some time or other. The idea of an individual attracting to himself this finer matter and assimilating it with his individuality may be compared to a man who should go into a smoky sooty atmosphere with his body oiled or greased; the grease would form the ground into which the particles of soot would sink; and if the man did not know the scientific way of removing it from his body, (by soap and water) he will have to wait until it wears off naturally; and so with the karma, if he does not know how to scientifically remove it, he will have to wait until it naturally wears off. (The way of removing it has been described roughly in the series of lectures on concentration).

We have in our nature impellent forces which are the ground so to speak on which foreign particles can rest and will be assimilated by the individual. As a magnet among an assortment of mental dust will attract to itself the iron filings, so there is a kind of magnetism in the individual which attracts and assimilates the foreign particles.

Points of view from which the Karma can be studied

The philosophy of karma may be studied from different points of view such as the nature of karma, the quality, the action, the kind of experience of pleasure or pain which it will give the individual. We may study it in reference to its intensity, and therefore the intensity with which they will manifest themselves. Or we may study karma in reference to the duration: it may stay for a thousand years or for five years. Or in reference to its mass, one may be heavy, another may be light. Or fifthly we may study how the karma is generated and how it manifests itself when ripe, how it can be worked out before its natural time, and incidentally though very important, how we can stop from the very beginning the inflow of karma. Prevention is better than cure.

Karma in reference to its nature, its action

From this point of view there are eight heads under which it may be classified. It can be classified into eight classes. Karma is always a foreign matter, it is always an obscuring element obscuring some quality of the soul; and the sooner it is worked out the better. When the karma is worked out, then the quality of the soul which was obscured, appears and becomes actual.

The most important karma refers to the very essence of the soul or individual (and that very essence is knowledge, consciousness, cognization). So that the first kind of karma is that which obscures the knowledge.

Classifications of the Karmas into 8 kinds

Class I. Knowledge obscuring karma [ज्ञानावरणीय]

Class 2. is that karma which obscures cognition in an undifferentiated way. Cognition in an undifferentiated way, that is a general cognition (of a horse for instance); it is the first stage of all consciousness; if this first activity does not take place, the soul does not know. You see a picture for instance, but you do not go into the details of it; you just know in a general way that it is a picture. The Sanskrit for this general is 'darshana'. [दर्शनावरणीय]

Class 3. is that karma the result of which is the feeling of either pain or pleasure. Knowledge by itself is not pain nor pleasure, but on account of certain karma in me, I feel pain or pleasure. Experiencing pain or pleasure is different from the consciousness or awareness of pain or pleasure. In consciousness there is no pain or pleasure, though at the time of pain or pleasure there may be consciousness of it. [वेदनीय]

Class 4. is that kind of karma which obstructs or acts as an obstacle to the formation of right belief and right conduct. Belief (conviction, that it is wrong to kill, for instance) is different from knowledge. In the worst form of this karma, we believe that which is wrong to be right, and that which is right to be wrong. A sub-division of this karma acts also as an obstacle to right conduct. The person does not intend to act in the right way, he does not intend, there is no intention to act. This karma is an obstacle to the very formation of an intention. [**मोहनीय**]

Class 5. is the karma which determines the duration of any particular life period, such as the life on this *planet* from birth to death. It is always generated in the incarnation just next before. [आयु :]

Class 6. is that karma which gives the living being the various factors of his objective individuality, voice, colour, features, etc. It makes him *Mr. Smith or Mr. Jones* ; his personality. [नाम]

Class 7. determines the surroundings, the family into which he is born, whether high or low. The birth into a certain family is not an accident, according to the Jain philosophy. It is determined by a certain kind of karma. There is really no such thing as 'accident', the word is only rightly used for those phenomena for which no explanation can be given; the Jain (*Sanskrit*) word for 'accident' means "I do not know from what it has taken place". [गोत्र]

Class 8. is the kind of karma which, like the 4th, also acts as an obstacle, but to different things; in the 4th there was no desire of acting in the right way; in this 8th there is the desire to do something good, to enjoy certain good things, but still, although you have the desire, certain obstacles come in the way, you cannot do it. [अन्तराय]

We must know how the karma is generated, how it is worked out before its time, how long it would stay with us, & c.

Karma is generated by reason of certain impellent forces within us, and these impellent forces need to be explained – impellent forces on account of the presence of which we generate the karma.

Darshana – the state where there is undifferentiated knowledge, formless knowledge; the limitations and boundaries are not fixed and you only know the thing as belonging to a class and not individualized.

SECOND LECTURE

In giving the doctrine of karma, the first thing to do is to classify the phenomena and then give the theory explaining the phenomena.

The function, nature, or action of each class of karma is quite different.

Class 1. is that karma the function of which is to obscure the knowing faculty, or to retard the development of the knowing faculty. There are words and thoughts, the tendency of which is to retard knowing. Karma is a peculiar force which we generate and the result of which ultimately acts on our individuality. In Sanskrit, this class of karma is called Gnânâvaraniya karma. (In Sanskrit the letter 'a' is pronounced like the letter 'u' in the word 'but'. And the letter 'â' is pronounced like the letter 'a' in the word 'calm').

Class 2. is that karma which obscures the general perceiving faculty. It is called Darshanávaraniya karma.

Class 3. is that karma by reason of which we have feelings of pains and pleasures. (Quite different from consciousness. In consciousness taken by itself there is neither pain nor pleasure; feeling is quite a distinct phenomena from consciousness). This karma is called Vedaniya karma.

Class 4. is called Mohaniya karma. (Literally, intoxicating karma, that is, mental, or moral intoxication.) Its nature is to infatuate our mental and moral nature, in such a way that we are not able to distinguish between right and wrong.

Class 5. Āyuh karma. (Literally, duration of life.) It determines the duration of the life and the general nature of the life. This karma generated in this life, determines what the next incarnation or rebirth will be like and its duration. (But it does not fix the number of years or months of life; it is rather 'quantity' of life than length; and as water can be squeezed out of a sponge quickly or slowly, so if this āyuh is used up quickly, the life in years will be a less number than if it be used up slowly or spun out).

Class 6. Nàma karma. Is that karma by reason of which we have our objective individuality. The combination of all the factors of individuality which when taken together makes us call a person *Mr-or Mrs-so-and-so.*

Class 7. Gotra karma. By reason of which the person is born into his particular social surroundings. (When people do not know the causes of things, they say it is accident, or Divine providence, or the act of God, or some expression which amounts to saying that they do not know the cause of the phenomenon).

Class 8. Antarâya karma. Literally, obstacle. Its nature is to throw obstacles in our way, should we want to do certain good things. It is not an accident, there are certain reasons, and the philosophy explains, why the person is unable to put forth the effort of the will.

Karma apart from an individual is nothing; it is a factor of the individual, it is in him; apart from him it is mere matter and has nothing to do with his individuality. Because that person acted in a certain way, and used certain words, or entertained certain thoughts with a certain object in view, he generated certain forces which became assimilated with his individuality and therefore, he is influenced by it. It is not a real separation; it is not a difference between the karma and the individual, it is the mode of behaviour of the individual. It is not entirely separate in fact from the person who generates it.

Impellent Forces, or Causes

It is not under all circumstances that a person's action or word, or thought would be the cause of the karma, it is only in certain circumstances. That is to say when the exercise of the different faculties of the person are preceded by certain impellent forces, or in other words, when by reason of certain impellent forces in him, a person says something or does something or thinks something, then he generates the karma.

These impellent forces are not the cause, because the cause is the person himself. The circumstantial causes are the instrumental causes, and these are his impellent forces. There are four kinds, namely, as follows –

1. **Delusion**. When a person is in that condition and does, thinks, or says something, then he generates karma. For instance, by way of illustration, when a man does not examine the belief into which he is born, as to its merits or demerits. Also doubts come under this heading. Again, when a man knows or believes that his doctrines are wrong and still preaches them, he generates a bad karma. Again, the state of delusion here meant is found

in those living beings in whom right belief does not exist, they, having formed no right or wrong beliefs; it is a state of the lack of development. Lack of development is injurious. The Sanskrit name of this first impellent force by reason of which, the karma is generated is Mithyâtva. (Mithyâ means wrong; and 'tva' means 'ness').

2. **Lack of control** over the senses and over the mental activities. The senses (taste, sight, etc.) are the channels of acquiring knowledge; and the indulging of the senses does not bring consciousness but stops it, you do not go further in thought about it. And if you have lack of control over the mental activity, when it is injurious to other people, when you do not or cannot stop injurious thoughts about another person, you generate a karma; the uncontrolled thought activity is the impellent force for the generation of karma. (The lecturer did not say, but I conclude that a tune persisting in the head against our will is an illustration very easy to recognize). The name of this impellent force is Avirati.

3. **Kashàya**. Literally, unclean moral nature. An unclean moral nature is the third impellent force by reason of which karma is generated.

4. **Yoga**. The word yoga has many meanings, but here it has a technical meaning, and means all other activities of body, mind, and speech which are not included in the first *three* forces mentioned, and it is therefore a general name. So that, certain karmas are generated by reason of the physiological activities. If a person is suffering from dispepsia, he perhaps loses his temper. Here is karma generated at once and manifested at once. So that, the philosophy of karma explains the injustice and inequalities in the world. We do

> sometimes generate the Karma even now and have the result the next moment. We are, as a matter of fact, generating karma every moment. (This was said by the lecturer, but might be *misleading*, because we can stop the inflow and we can work out all the karmas and finally become a liberated soul, which will appear later on).

The impellent force is called in Sanskrit Hetu. It signifies 'the means by which', 'the instrumental cause'.

The Karmas

We have had eight classes of karmas mentioned, with a rough description of their nature or function; and four kinds of causes or impellent forces which are the means of generating the karmas. We now come again to the eight classes of karmas.

Class 1. Knowledge obscuring karma. Certain acts and words and thoughts have the tendency to retard the faculty of knowing. In what different ways do we know ? We must classify the various forms of knowledge, then we can know that those forces which obscure the growth or manifestation of the different form of knowledge, are the very karmas which have been called the first class. The nature of this first class could not be understood unless we understand the different ways in which the function of knowing manifests itself. (There are as many forms of knowledge as there are living beings, as no two persons' knowledge is alike; but still we can classify the kinds).

The first form of knowledge, which is the basis of all phenomena of consciousness and of all activities of mind, is the knowledge based on the senses, including the knowledge based on the activity of the mind. And this form of knowledge, is called in the Jain philosophy (मीत) Mutijnâna; that is, sensuous knowledge plus something else. The initial stages of sensuous knowledge are knowledge; sensation is a degree of knowledge. It is not the bundle of sensations that make up knowledge, but it is the sensations in the higher form. There is a kind of Mutijnâna which does not depend upon reading or hearing. The cause of the presence of the knowledge is not to be found in anything that person has done in this life, but by reason of something he has done in a previous life. (For instance, if upon seeing a gas stove for the first time he at once understands it.) Then again, the moral nature helps to give a knowledge; and also with age the person is able to do better than he did in the early part of life, which improvement is not the result of study or reading.

And also there is the Mutijnâna which is the result of study or reading.

The second form of knowledge is (श्रुतज्ञान) Shrûtajnâna. Knowledge derived through reading, study. Knowledge derived from the interpreting of symbols or signs. Words are symbols of ideas. Knowledge derived from any kind of sign. If a dog sees his master wave his hand, the dog interprets the sign and knows that his master wants him to come. This is a higher form or channel of knowledge than the first, but still it is based on sensation: if we do not first see or hear or feel the sign we cannot interpret it.

The third form of knowledge is called (अवधी) Avadhi. It depends entirely upon the activity of the ego without the activity of the mind or the senses; and still it is knowledge limited in extent and content.

The fourth form of knowledge is (मनःपर्यव) Manah-paryava-jnāna; or mind-knowing.

The fifth form of knowledge is (केवल) Kevala; or omniscience, knowledge which has no limitations as to space or time or subject.

The first two forms of knowledge are the only two recognized in the West and it is in this stage that most people are.

Memory, judgment, perception, etc., are the results of the removal of knowledge obscuring karmas.

THIRD LECTURE

The consciousness of the individual is not identical with the physiological activity of the body; the one may even be dependent upon, but it is different from the other. Consciousness is one thing, activity of brain molecules is another different thing.

Knowledge, when it is right, true and corresponds to the facts, is the essential quality of the soul; it is that which would be manifested if there were no mistakes; the cause of mistakes in the knowledge obscuring karma; owing to karma we make mistakes in perceiving, judging, etc.

Anything that takes place on account of the joint action of the soul and the karma is, from the ideal standpoint, the unnatural condition of the soul.

There was not any particular time in the past when this entity called the soul was without any karmas; because if we assume that there was then it follows that after taking the trouble to remove the karmas through mental and moral disciplines, after going through a lot of ordeals, we might again come into combination with karmas. The fundamental basis of the philosophy is that, so far as the past is concerned, there was not any time when the soul was without any Karma.

The combination of the soul and the karma is not a mechanical mixture, separable by simply taking apart as a coat from the body. The combination of the soul with karma is a subtle combination, and can be seen thus: in a mechanical mixture the substances are only in juxtaposition, such as sugar and water, and you can seperate one from the other readily. Then there is chemical combination, when two or more substances unite to that the compound cannot be seen in its elements; water, for instance, is a compound of hydrogen and oxygen, and these in combination make water, which is a quite different substance from either, and neither hydrogen nor oxygen can be seen in it. So it is with the combination of the soul with karma, the combination is even more subtle than the chemical combination, and the result is a different substance from either of the ingredients.

The soul is a supersensuous substance; *in thought*, it can be divided into parts, but not actually; it cannot be actually taken apart.

To reduce the combination of soul and karma, you have to use certain mental and moral disciplines.

Each state of the soul had a beginning (that is, any one given particular state, it was always in the past combined with karma, but its combination with any particularly mentioned or given karma at a particularly mentioned time – this particular state had its beginning); but the soul itself, which is the subject of these states, had no beginning. There never was a first state, in the sense of their being no previous one.

It is unnatural for the soul part of the compound (with anger, for instance, which is a karma) to act in an angry manner. We commonly hear it said of a person, that he acted in anger, he was *not himself*.

There will be a time in the future, when the soul is without karma; and once without it will always thereafter henceforth be without, perfect and liberated.

In every activity of a living being in the embodied state, there are two sides, an objective and a subjective side. In the activity of sensation, there are the two sides, the objective side and the subjective side (internal side), the objective organs of sensation (eyes, nose, etc.), and the subjective organs of sensation, each having many subdivisions.

When consciousness is only re-presenting something to itself or comparing ideas, then another instrument has to be used, and this is 'manas' (mind), and it is only found in living beings having five organs of sensation. (As before mentioned, this doctrine of karma applies to all living beings, and not merely to man). The mind has also two sides, objective and subjective.

All knowledge itself has two aspects or points of view, namely the right and the wrong. One person forms a judgment, perhaps, about another person, and it is a wrong judgment. And until we get the habit or the ability of assuming the right attitude, we cannot form right judgments.

With reference to the first form of knowledge, or mutijnâna, we now come to the different stages of this form of knowledge; the process.

There are five stages in the process, namely;

1. In this first stage, what takes place is the establishment of the relation of contact between the organs of sensation and the vibrations from the external object in the external world. The stimulus from outside, create a sort of excitation in the end-organ (ear, eye, etc.) – only in the organs of sensation and not in the mind. In this first stage a relation is established between the subjective and objective world.
2. After the relation is established, a kind of excitation takes place in the consciousness, where the person thinks "What is that" ? This second stage, in the process, is the first activity of the mind, (manas). It is the state of mind in which the person asks himself "What is that" ? or "What was that" ? when recalling something seen or heard in the past.
3. Then after the mind has thus been aroused, there follow three more stages in the process of knowing the object.

The mind itself does not come into contact with the physical object and does not pass through the above mentioned in first stage; still it has the second stage. In the third stage now being mentioned the consciousness begins to run in this way – (suppose I see something in the distance which I cannot quite make out) "What is this"? well, it cannot be a person, still it has that shape, and yet it does not move, etc. It is a kind of cogitation. There is the consciousness of similarities and differences.

4. And then you come to the fourth stage. It is the conclusion. "No, it is a tree stump" and "not a human being". (Western psychologies would say that all this is the activity of the mind).

5. In this stage a kind of process goes on, in the consciousness of the individual, and the result of the process is the preservation to a more or less extent of the consciousness acquired in this way. A modification of the consciousness has taken place and will last a certain length of time; and this lasting quality is called this 5th name 'Dhâranâ'. (The names of the previous stages are given below). This last stage manifests in the form of the continuance for a certain length of time of the new knowledge. It may also manifest itself in the form which results in only certain impressions made on our consciousness – on account of the impressions the life of the individual is so changed that the activities will in future be different. And a third way in which the last stage of the process of mutijnāna manifests itself is that the thing (the thing newly known) can be remembered – it is memory. Memory, as a faculty, is the last result of the activities, which are classed under mutijnâna or the first form of knowledge.

All, except the first stage of these five stages of the process, are the activities of the mind (manas).

The obscuring karma being removed, the quality of the soul called memory is able to manifest itself.

Any activity of the individual which lessens the capacity of the organs of sensation or of the mind to pass through any of these stages, is knowledge obscuring karma, and each person must discover these karmas or activities for himself, otherwise he does not know what the karmas are, simply to tell him that there are knowledge obscuring karmas is to tell him nothing.

The names of the above mentioned stages are:

1. Vyanjana avagraha
2. Artha avagraha
3. Īhâ
4. Avaya
5. Dhâranâ

The following is in my notes taken at the time of the lecture: Throughout the whole process, the working of the mutijnâna is dependent upon the interpretive faculty, either of the words of a language, or of the actions of the hands and body, etc. There are two kinds of mutijnâna, one which is based and one which is not based on this interpretive faculty.

With reference to the statement above, that each state of the soul had a beginning, I asked the question "If each state had a beginning, then it follows that the state of being in combination with karma, must have had a beginning and yet it was said that the state of being with karma had no beginning. How are these statements reconciled?" I received the answer and saw the solution. The question arises from ambiguity in the meaning of the word 'state'. The particular state in which the soul is at any given date and place did have a beginning. The state of existence, if 'existence' can be called a state, it should rather be called a 'fact'; the 'fact' of existence did not have a beginning; there never was a time when the individual soul did not exist in some state and in some place.

FOURTH LECTURE

It is the classification of the karmas from the point of view of their nature or function that is now being given. Class I has been called knowledge obscuring karma or Jnanāvaraniya karma. And as there are five forms of knowledge, as already mentioned, so there are five subdivisions of this Class I, namely, karma which obscures either the mutijnāna, the shrutajnāna, the avadhi, the manah-paryava-jnāna, or the kevala-jnāna.

This detailed classification of the karmas, or rather the subdivisions of the 8 Classes, continues now up to the end of the lecture No. 9; Class I is subdivided into 5 subdivisions; Class 2 into 9 subdivisions; Class 3 into 2 subdivisions; Class 4 into 28 subdivisions; Class 5 into 4 subdivisions; Class 6 into 103 subdivisions; Class 7 into 2 subdivisions; Class 8 into 5 subdivisions.

To continue with the subdivisions of Class No. I.

Subdivision the 2nd: is that karma which obscures the second form of knowledge (shrutajnāna). Shrutajnāna is knowledge acquired by interpreting signs; to know through signs is shrutajnāna. Reading is interpreting signs; there are the signs by which we know that a man is angry; a man sneezing, is a sign, that there is something the matter with his nervous system.

Subdivision the 3rd: is that karma which obscures the form of knowledge known as 'avadhijnāna'. In this form of knowledge the soul or ego comes to know about material objective things and beings without the use of the sense-organs or the mind. It is the next higher form of knowing after shrutajnāna. The karma which obscures this form of knowing is active in nearly all of us. By this means of knowing we become aware of physical things at a distance without going to the place or having the sense-organs in contact with the object. So that, while in London you know what is going on in New York, or in Mars, or on the Sun. But it is only material matters that are known by this means (as distinguished from ideas or thoughts, as referred to in the following or 4th form of knowing). There is just the following (few rough particulars) given about the kinds of this avadhi-jnāna:

(a) The kind which follows you from place to place, so that you have this way of knowing in whatever town or place you may be.

(b) The kind which is with you only at a certain town or place and nowhere else, so that if you leave that town, you lose the ability to know in this way.

(c) The kind which is increasing, so that as time goes on, you are able to more and more know by this means.

(d) The kind which decreases every moment, so that as time goes on, you are able less and less to know by this means, until it may disappear.

(e) When you have just one flash of knowing in this way during the life, and no more, either before or after.

(f) When it comes it stays. You get it and keep it.

Subdivision the 4th: is that karma which obscures the form of knowing called 'Manah-paryava-jnāna. It is mind knowing; you know the other person's mind, what the ideas and the thoughts are. In the avadhi, you may see the mental pictures which the thoughts of the man produce, but you do not know his real thoughts or mind. Things and objects can be seen, but thoughts cannot be seen, they can be known. You know an idea, you do not literally see it. In this form of knowing you actually know the thoughts of people. Of course it is obscured in us, and is not recognized as a way of knowing in the West.

Subdivision the 5th: is that karma which obscures the form of knowing called Kevala-jnāna, knowledge which is quite unlimited and disembodied.

Thus in Class No. I of the 8 classes of karma there are the above mentioned 5 subdivisions.

With reference to the avadhi-jnāna, it was said in illustration of the (e) kind that a pupil of a teacher had the perception by this means of some man and wife in a distant planet and being amused with what they were doing, the pupil smiled and laughed, and then the sight disappeared. The teacher said that the act of laughing stopped the knowing. In laughing he left off knowing.

The knowing faculty is one aspect of the pure soul. There are other aspects, but knowing is one.

From the low standpoint (see later on under Nigoda) the karma is a higher stage; from the ideal standpoint the karma is an obstruction: the stage of karma is a stage in the line of progress of the soul from the low standpoint.

Subdivision of Class 2
(Darshanāvaraniya karma)

Darshana, as already mentioned, means detailless knowledge, you simply know a thing as belonging to a class, without going into its attributes or ways of behaving: in Jnāna (knowledge) you know the ins and outs to some extent. Detailed knowledge is Jnāna. There are the following 9 subdivisions of this 2nd Class of Karma, namely:

1. Karma which obscures the Darshana, (there is no one English word which will correctly translate this word) which is received through the eye.

2. Karma which obscures the darshana received through any sense other than the eye (ear, nose, tongue, or skin).
3. Karma which obscures the avadhi (there is no equivalent English word) darshana.
4. Karma which obscures the Kevala darshana. In the following five states the senses are not active, and therefore you do not see, or hear, or smell &c. The sleep states in their various degrees are among these states.
5. Sleep from which a person can be awakened without any trouble, simply by calling his name; he will hear his name but will not hear other conversation or sounds.
6. Sleep in which you have to touch the body of the person in order to awaken him; it is strong sleep; the consciousness has been fatigued so much that it requires a fair stimulus to wake the man up.
7. The consciousness goes to sleep while the body is sitting – a very strong degree of sleep.
8. Sleep while walking (known sometimes of soldiers on the march).
9. The somnambulistic state; this is the worst form of this kind of karma (of darshanāvaraniya karma). Āvaraniya means obscuring or preventing. This also includes the hypnotic state.

The higher you rise in advancement the more you have the consciousness of your thoughts, of your actions and of every activity through which you pass. The less you are conscious of these things in the downward direction you are going.

With regard to the avadhi lately mentioned where the soul comes to know directly of distant things without the use of the eye or ear etc, this avadhi must take place in the waking state, while the eye and ear etc, are there and awake, this avadhi is not any kind of dream or trance state, it takes place in the ordinary waking state, when one is up and about.

FIFTH LECTURE

Subdivisions of Class 3

There are two subdivisions of this karma, namely as follows:

1. Karma which in its working, causes feelings of pain.
2. Karma which in its working, causes feelings of pleasure.

It is necessary for a distinction to be made between 'feelings of pain or pleasure' and such feelings as pride, grief, anger, and others. Feelings of pain and pleasure do not necessarily hinder the progress of the soul; feelings of pride, anger, etc. do; but if you identify yourself with a pain or a pleasure you come to a stop, you do not continue in the right strain. The name of this 3rd class of karma is, Vedaniya karma.

Subdivisions of Class 4

There are 28 subdivisions of this kind of karma, but these 28 can be classified under two heads, namely, the first 3 are called darshana mohaniya karmas, whose nature is to obstruct the faculty of relishing the truth when it is heard. And the remaining 25 are called châritra mohaniya karmas, whose nature is, to obstruct right conduct. You may relish it and still you cannot practise it; you perhaps feel weak and so do not practise the truth which is relished.

The Darshana Mohaniya karmas are;

1. That karma by reason of the activity of which you do not believe in the truth at all when it is presented to you; the person is entirely under the rule of delusion.

2. That karma by reason of which you believe for some time and then there is a doubt you are all the time vacillating.
3. That karma by reason of which, while believing in the truth all the time still at certain moments you feel that there is something more to be known. There is just a little vacillating in this state.

The Chāritra Mohaniya karmas are;

1. Anger of an intense degree,
2. Anger of a less intense degree,
3. Anger of a milder degree,
4. Anger of a still milder degree,
5. Pride of an intense degree,
6. Pride of a less intense degree,
7. Pride of a milder degree,
8. Pride of a still milder degree,
9. Deceitfulness of an intense degree,
10. Deceitfulness of a less intense degree,
11. Deceitfulness of a milder degree,
12. Deceitfulness of a still milder degree,
13. Greed of an intense degree,
14. Greed of a less intense degree,
15. Greed of a milder degree,
16. Greed of a still milder degree,
17. Laughing and joking,
18. Confirmed improper liking (liking without looking to the merits of the thing liked),
19. Confirmed improper disliking,
20. Sorrow, or grief (which would include worry),

21. Fear (nearly all wrong action can ultimately be traced to fear),
22. Disgust,
23. The male sex passion,
24. The female sex passion,
25. The neuter sex passion.

This completes the list of the 28 kinds of the Class 4 or Mohaniya karma, the nature of which is to intoxicate or infatuate the mind in such a way that it cannot distinguish between right and wrong belief or conduct. Now follows a more detailed description of them.

Anger: The four degrees of anger may be compared respectively to first the split in the side of a mountain, it will be there the whole life time; anger causes separation between persons and in this which is the most intense degree the anger is so great towards the person, that you feel you can never be friendly or amiable towards him (or her). This is merely the description of the degree of anger, of course, by an effort of will and understanding it can be overcome. The next degree which is less intense, may be compared to splits in clay; they will remain until rain falls and, moistening the clay, the splits will be joined together. You may be angry with a person until somebody else comes and makes peace by talking and showing or explaining the folly of anger. The next degree may be compared to ruts on sand, they will remain until the wind blows the sand together; and the mild degree of anger can be compared to a line made in water, with a stick; the joint is effected as soon as the dividing instrument is withdrawn; in this degree the anger is checked by the mind, the moment it is felt to be rising.

Pride: The most intense degree may be compared to a pillar of stone, you can never make it bend, the man never yields, not when he is wrong, and is not tolerant, his obstinacy is very great (when he is in the wrong is meant). The less intense degree may be compared to a bone, it is difficult to bend it; it is only with great difficulty that the person who has this degree of pride, will yield to certain things which he ought to yield to. The next degree upwards, may be compared to a dry piece of wood, if you apply oil, or soak it in water for sometime then it bends, but still not very easily. The next degree is like a cane, you can bend it at once, the person yields at once to the right. Pride is like a mountain in front of one, it hides the view, it obscures knowledge, we do not see beyond that which is immediately in front of us.

Deceitfulness: Its chief characteristic is crookedness; the conflict between the thought and the action. The first or worst degree may be compared to the knot in bamboo, you cannot make it straight. The next to the horns of sheep, it is with great difficulty that they can be straightened. The next to the course of water from a sprinkling can, it will be there so long as the water is there but it will dry up and then the crookedness will be gone (the wave line of water). The next to shavings of wood, they are bent but you can straighten them at once. Deceit prevents right belief about people.

Greed: The chief characteristic is attachment or clinging to; it is the identifying of the self with the not-self. (I think it was to illustrate this that the lecturer said when my child broke a cup and saucer the other day I got angry and yet half a dozen cups may break and I not feel injured or get angry about it). (The character is not injured by such losses, the moral nature; but it is injured by the anger). The worst degree of greed may be compared to fast dye, it cannot be removed, and it will last the whole life time. Next to grease from a cartwheel hub, it is very difficult to remove. Next to colour which can be washed off with soap and water. Next to colour that can be washed off with water, you put it in water and the colour is off.

These qualities of anger, pride, deceitfulness and greed are qualities in a man's nature by virtue of which he cannot act rightly. Now there are nine more, namely:

Laughing and Joking: When we are in this mood, we are not in the straight line of the acquisition of truth; it stops the right action and the right attitude.

Improper and Confirmed Pre-Judicial Liking: Such as 'party' spirit, which upholds the political party whether right or wrong; favouritism, etc., it is when the merits and demerits are not regarded.

Improper and Confirmed Pre-Judicial Dislikings: Same as the previous, only disliking instead of liking.

Sorrow: Sorrow is an obstacle to right conduct, because in the state of sorrow the actions are only such as are injurious. There is also the tendency to unjustly accuse other people, when in sorrow.

Fear: Fear stops right action, very many wrong actions can be ultimately traced to fear. Fear is replaced by the desire to do good to others, by sympathy; the more there is of benevolence the less there is of fear.

Disgust: Disgust is an obstruction to knowledge and to right action. Instead of going further into the matter, you are disgusted and stop knowing about it; there should be the recognition that the thing can only exist in those circumstances. A disgusting smell of decaying fish, for instance.

Sex Passion: The sex passion that is to be found in men; the sex passion that is to be found among women; and the sex passion that is to be found in those who have no sexual signs; but still they have the passion and theirs is the strongest of all. When a person is under the influence of the sexual passion, he is not conscious of what is right and what is wrong.

So we have 28 mohaniya karmas; they can be compared to an alcoholic liquor; they intoxicate.

SIXTH LECTURE

As the karmas are foreign substances obscuring the qualities of the soul, it follows that upon the removal of them the soul's qualities become actual.

That quality of the soul, which appears when the Class I karma is removed, is unlimited knowledge (omniscience). When the Vedaniya or Class 3 karma is removed, then the quality of the soul which appears is permanent bliss; the Vedaniya karma obscures the bliss quality of the soul. When the Class 4 or Mohaniya karma is worked out, then there is always light belief and right conduct, we always form right beliefs and always act rightly. This point follows in proper order after the details of the remaining classes of karma.

Subdivisions of Class 5

This karma is called Ayuh karma. It determines how long we live in a particular body; it may be compared with fetters; it prevents the realisation of the spiritual continuous life, and after this karma is removed, the soul lives in its own body and not in any physical or karmic body. There are four subdivisions of the Ayuh karma, namely:

1. That karma by reason of which the person lives for a length of time (it may be a billion years) in the pleasurable condition, known as the Devas, having a fine subtle body.
2. That karma by reason of which the person lives for a length of time (it may be a billion years) in the lower subtle body condition, in which there is no pleasure at

all; but pain all the time. It is called the Naraka condition.

3. That karma by reason of which, the person lives in the human state with a physical body. It is called Manushāyuh-karma.

4. Fourth is that karma by reason of which, the entity lives as an animal, with a body as found among animals. (This includes worms, birds, vegetables, bears, etc.) Tiryanchāyuh-karma.

The Āyuh karma determines the state, in which the entity has to stay, and is caused by the words, and thoughts, and actions in the previous life immediately next backwards.

Subdivisions of Class 6

There are 103 subdivisions of this karma. It is called Nāma karma (Name karma). It gives the personality; and when destroyed or rather removed, the soul does not pass through these mixed phases of matter and spirit; when worked out, the nature of the individual is the same all the time, his personality is fixed, and it is a continuous life, a soul in the purest condition. The 103 kinds are grouped as follows:

14 which are called 'Collective karmas', the collective stuff of the various karmas.

8 which are called 'pratyeka prakriti' karmas.

10 which is a collection called 'trasa dashaka'.

10 which is a collection called 'sthāvara dashaka'.

But this only makes 42, but the first 14 are by smaller subdivisions made into 75.

The first 75 subdivisions, then, of the nāma karma are as follows, and to assist in grasping them, it can be remembered that they consist of 14 groups, and the whole 75 are called 'collective' or Pinda prakriti.

GROUP I

4 Gati nāma karmas, namely:

1. Deva gati nāma karma, is that karma that brings the living being into that state of existence, known as the Deva state; it is a pleasureable state in a fine subtle body, perhaps comparable to the Christian heaven. It is a state, in which pleasure preponderates over pain, there is some pain but mostly pleasure.
2. Naraka gati nāma karma, is that karma which brings the living being into the naraka state; where there is no pleasure at all, but pain all the time, perhaps comparable to the Christian hell. (But it is not everlasting, it comes to an end).
3. Manushya gati nāma karma, is that karma which brings the living being into the human state, our ordinary human life.
4. Tiryancha gati nāma karma, is that karma which brings the living being into the animal state (animal, insect, fish, bird, vegetable, or mineral life).

GROUP 2

5 Jāti nāma karmas

5. That karma by reason of which the living being has the sense of touch.
6. That karma by reason of which the living being has the senses of touch and taste. (If a living being has only one sense, it is always the sense of touch; if two only, it is always touch and taste, and so on with the following).
7. That karma by reason of which the living being has the senses of touch, taste, and smell.

8. That karma by reason of which the living being has the senses of touch, taste, smell, and sight.
9. That karma by reason of which the living being has the senses of touch, taste, smell, sight, and hearing. (Vegetables would have only one organ of sense, the sense of touch).

GROUP 3

5 Sharira nāma karmas, namely:

10. Audārika sharira nāma karma, is that karma by reason of which the living being has the ordinary physical body, that we actually see.
11. Vaiknya sharira nāma karma, by reason of the activity of this karma, the living being has a subtle body, which is changeable; it may be large and then small, have one shape and then another. The beings in the state of Deva and in the state of Naraka have this body, and not a physical body.
12. Āhāraka sharira nāma karma, gives a body that can be sent by the person to a Master. It is only very advanced beings that have this body.
13. Taijasa sharira nāma karma, gives a body which consumes food, and when highly developed and rendered more subtle it can be protruded from the person and consume or burn up other things or persons or bodies.
14. Kārmana sharira nāma karma, gives the body which is made up of all the karmas put together. It is changing every moment.

Of these five bodies, we all of us, here have the physical, the digesting body, and the kārmana body. We may or may not have the subtle or vaikriya body, while only the very spiritually advanced have the āharāka body.

GROUP 4

3 Upānga nāma karmas, namely:

15. Audārika Upānga nāma karma, is that karma, on account of which the limbs and organs of the physical body are formed, internal and external organs, arms, legs, ears, lungs etc.
16. Vaikriya upānga nāma karma, would form the limbs and organs of the subtle or vaikriya body.
17. Āhāraka upānga nāma karma, produces the limbs of the āhāraka body.

The taijasa and the kārmana bodies do not have limbs or organs.

GROUP 5

15 Bandhana nāma karmas, namely:

18. Audārika bandhana nāma karma, this karma, when it is working, binds together the different parts of the physical body, it is the assimilation karma; the activity of this karma mixes the foreign matter and makes it one lump, changing its nature.
19. Vaikriya bandhana nāma karma, same as the previous one, only applying to the subtle body instead of the physical body.
20. Āhāraka bandhana nāma karma, same thing only for the āhāraka body.
21. Taijasa bandhana nāma karma, same thing for the taijasa body.
22. Kārmana bandhana nāma karma, for the kārmana body.

23-32. Then by other combinations of two and sometimes of three of the kinds of matters, ten more kinds are produced, but it is unnecessary to give them.

GROUP 6

5 Sanghatana nāma karmas, namely:

33. Audārika sanghatana nāma karma, by reason of the activity of which you rake in as it were from the outside or rake together the matter for the physical body. Literally it means 'collecting', or 'bringing together'. That which collects materials from outside to form the eye etc.; this karma works outside and brings things together into heaps as it were.
34. Vaikriya sanghatana nāma karma, same as the previous, only for the vaikriya or subtle body.
35. Āhāraka sanghatana nama karma, for the āhāraka body.
36. Taijasa, the same as the previous for the taijasa body.
37. Kārmana sanghatana nāma karma, for the kārmana body.

GROUP 7

6 Samhanana nāma karmas, namely:

38. The function of this karma is to join the bones together, and this particular karma gives a peculiarly strong joint. It is the highest form of joint. The ends of the bones are hooked into each other, there is a sort of bolt or pin through the hook, and the whole joint is covered with an envelope of tissue. It is called Vajra-rishabha-nārāch-asamhanana nāma karma. Vajra means the 'pin'.
39. Rishabha-nārācha-samhanana nāma karma. The same as the previous one, only without the pin.

40. Nārācha-samhanana nāma karma, same as the previous only with the envelope omitted. Only the hook remains.

41. Ardha-nārācha samhanana nāma karma. The bones are at one end hooked into each other, and pinned, with no envelope, while at the other end, the bone is simply straight and pinned.

42. Kilika-samhanana nāma karma. The bones are straight at each end and nailed. No hook and no envelope.

43. Chhevaththhu samhanana nāma karma. This karma gives a joint where the bones simply touch, or are in sockets. Most of ours are like this; it is the weakest and worst form of joint. The teaching is that the greatest degree of concentration can only be attained in a body, having the first mentioned joints (Vajra &c.).

GROUP 8

6 Samsthāna nāma karmas, namely:

44. Sama-chatur-āsra-samsthāna nāma karma. By reason of this karma, the body is symmetrical,

45. Nyagrodha samsthāna nāma karma, by reason of this karma, the upper part of the body is symmetrical and the lower part is not. The lower part is defective by reason of this karma.

46. Sādi samsthāna nāma karma. By reason of which the lower part of the body is symmetrical, but the upper part is not.

47. Kubja samsthāna nama karma. The trunk is deformed by reason of this karma, while the legs, arms, face, neck are symmetrical. (Humpback, for instance.)

48. Vāmana samsthāna nāma karma, by reason of this karma the arms and legs are defective, while the trunk is all right (dwarf).

49. Hundā smasthāna nāma karma, by reason of which everything is unsymmetrical. The bodies of animals, fish, birds, insects come under this class, the human form being considered as the symmetrical form.

All beings born in the womb may have any of these six kinds of bodies; those living beings not born in the womb can have only the hundā body.

GROUP 9

5 Varna nāma karmas, namely:

50. By reason of the activity of this karma the living being is black or blue black.
51. By reason of this karma he (it) is green.
52. By reason of which the being is yellow.
53. By reason of which the being is red.
54. By reason of which the being is white-fair.

Of the above colours, the 1 and 2 are inferior, (though in respect to things other than colour the person may be superior), and the 3, 4, and 5 are superior colours. It does not follow that because a person is inferior in this one particular that he is therefore inferior in all, or if superior, superior in all. A white man may be a thief and a murderer; a black man may be virtuous, and spiritually advanced.

GROUP 10

2 Gandha nāma karmas, namely:

55. That karma which makes the general odor of the body pleasant.
56. That karma which makes the general odor of the body unpleasant.

GROUP 11

5 Rasa nāma karmas, namely:

57. By reason of this karma the body, if tasted, would be like pepper – that is hot, but not fire heat.
58. The body if tasted would be bitter.
59. The body if tasted would be astringent.
60. The body if tasted would be sour.
61. The body if tasted would be sweet.

GROUP 12

8 Sparsha nāma karmas, namely:

62. That karma which makes the body feel heavy.
63. That karma which makes the body feel light.
64. Which makes the body feel smooth.
65. Which makes the body feel rough.
66. Which makes the body feel cold.
67. Which makes the body feel warm.
68. Which makes the body feel oily.
69. Which makes the body feel dry.

GROUP 13

4 Anupurvi nāma karmas, namely:

70. That karma by which the direction of the living being, at death, is determined towards the place of the Devas. (There must be some force which causes the person at death to travel in the right direction to reach his next destination, whether to another planet or elsewhere, and it is this karma).

71. That karma which determines the direction of the living being at death towards the place of the Narakas.
72. That karma which determines the right direction of travel at death, for the entity to go to the place of the human beings.
73. That karma which determines the right direction of travel at death, for the entity to go to the place of the animals, (tiryanchas).

GROUP 14

2 Vihyo gati nāma karmas, namely:

74. That karma by reason of which the gait is bad. (As for instance, when the feet are turned inwards and are dragged along shuffling).
75. That karma by reason of which the gait is good.

That completes the first batch of 14 groups of 'collective' personality or nāma karma. Now follow three more batches, namely of 8, 10 and 10 respectively, namely;

8 Pratyeka prakriti nāma karmas

76. Parāghāta nāma karma, by the reason of this karma the person does not get conquered or beaten.
77. Utchchhvāsa nāma karma, by reason of the activity of which, the person is able to breathe fully. To the extent that this karma is weak the person is not able to breathe.
78. Ātapa nāma karma, its nature is to give a kind of warm luster and to make others feel a warmth in the presence of the person, (not always pleasant), though the person himself does not feel this warmth. We may feel overawed in the presence of that person.
79. Udyōta nāma karma, gives a bright luster, but it is cool,

not warm as the previous one was, so that you feel at home with the person.

80. Agurulaghu nāma karma, makes the body neither heavy nor light.

81. Tirthankara nāma karma, is that karma by the generation of which and through the activity of which the person in some incarnation becomes a Master.

82. Nirmāna nāma karma, by reason of which the different organs and limbs of the body come to be in the right places.

83. Upaghāta nāma karma, by reason of which the organs are placed in such a way that instead of getting the normal pleasures from the normal activities, we get pain. This karma brings functional disorders so that in the function of the organ pain is produced. (This karma has some relation with the Vedaniya or pain karma).

10 Trasa dashaka (Dashaka means ten)

84. Trasa nāma karma, technically means (the word trasa, that is) a living being who can move about voluntarily–bees, fish, birds, animals, etc. By reason of the activity of this karma the living being passes from a stationary state (tree, for instance) to a state in which the body has voluntary motions.

85. Bâdara nāma karma, by reason of which karma, the living being passes from a body which is so minute as to be invisible to a body, which is large enough to be visible.

86. Paryāpta nāma karma, paryāpta means capability. Through the activity of this karma, the living being has the capacity to complete the construction of the various bodily parts and capacities; the capability to fully develop them. There are various capacities, for instance, to take food from the outside, to assimilate it

with the body, etc. etc. He has the capability to complete these capacities by reason of this karma.

87. Pratyeka nāma karma, is that karma by reason of which, a living being obtains an individual body, a body for itself. There are living beings having a common body, so that many may be living in one body, such as vegetables growing underground.

88. Sthira nāma karma, by reason of which, the teeth and bones are quite strong, solid, substantial and coherent.

89. Shubha nāma karma, by reason of which the upper part of the whole body is symmetrical. There is a difference between this and the nyagrodha samsthāna nāma karma; in this shubha karma the point is that the upper part of the body *pleases* other people, and also the lower part need not necessarily be defective. In the nyagrodha karma the point is that the construction is symmetrical, and the lower part must be defective.

90. Saubhayya nāma karma, an activity by reason of which the person becomes quite popular.

91. Susvara nāma karma, by reason of which the voice is musical.

92. Ādeya nāma karma, by reason of which the person's words obtain weight among people, he is believed.

93. Yashah kirti nāma karma, by reason of which the person becomes famous. (In the good sense).

The following last ten of the nāma karmas are the counterparts of the ten karmas just mentioned, 10 Stāvara dashaka.

94. Stāvara nāma karma, this is the contrary of the first karma of the previous ten (counterpart just above is wrong, it is the contraries). By reason of this karma, the living being goes to a stationary body.

95. Sukshma nāma karma, which makes the body so small that it cannot be seen by the eyes.
96. Aparyāpta nāma karma, by reason of this karma, the living being does not complete the body, and dies.
97. Sādhārana nāma karma, the living being occupies a common body; one body for many living beings (potato, for instance).
98. Asthira nāma karma, the teeth and bones are not fixed and coherent.
99. Ashubha nāma karma, the upper part of the body is not symmetrical or pleasing, is not of a kind which pleases others.
100. Daurbhāgya nāma karma, by reason of this karma he is unpopular, whether he is doing good or ill to the people.
101. Duhsvara nāma karma, the voice is not musical.
102. Anādeya nāma karma, by reason of which the person is not believed, even though he is speaking the truth; his words do not carry weight.
103. Apayashah-apakirti nāma karma, by reason of which there is disrepute (the opposite of fame).

That completes the list of the 103 nāma karmas. All these karmas can be changed and improved.

Subdivisions of Class 7

The name of this class is Gotra karma, there are only two subdivisions, namely;

1. Uchcha gotra karma, which brings the living being, into high family surroundings.
2. Nicha Gotra karma, by reason of which the living being is born into low family and social circumstances.

Subdivisions of Class 8

The name is Antaraya karma. Literally 'obstacle' karma. This karma acts as an obstacle to that which you desire to do. In the mohaniya (class 4) the inability to act rightly is owing to moral depravity (or uncleanness, rather; depravity implies a previous time of non-depravity, whereas the living being may always in the past have been of an unclean moral nature), and consequent non-perception of what is right; whereas in the antaraya karma the right action is seen, but is not done. There are five kinds of this antaraya karma, namely;

1. Dānāntarāya karma 'dāna' means to give. By reason of this karma the person is obstructed or prevented from giving, although it is the right time and place, and he has the means, still he does not give.
2. Lābhāntarāya karma, 'lābh' means gain. This karma is that which is an obstacle to gain or profit. The person is a fit person and follows the usual methods of gaining and yet does not gain.
3. Bhogāntarāya karma, 'bhog' means enjoyment. This karma prevents the enjoying of objects or things which can be enjoyed more than once; pictures, scenery, furniture, etc. etc. The things themselves are not faulty and yet the person is miserable although surrounded by enjoyable things.
4. Upabhogāntarāya karma, upa means less or sub. This karma prevents the enjoying of things which can be enjoyed only once; a cake, a glass of wine, etc. eating and drinking.
5. Viryāntarāya karma, Viry (pronounced veeri) means force or power, the will to do. This karma acts as an obstacle to the will power, you would like to do the thing but still you cannot; you know that it is right yet you cannot do it; there is weakness.

This 8th class or antarāya karma is one which covers up one aspect of the real spiritual nature of the soul, so that the goodness is not actual, it is not done actually. (Well meaning is nothing, the intellect and the life must be improved).

Out of these 8 kinds of karma, these 8 classes that is, there are four which do and four which do not cover up the real spiritual nature of the soul, those which do cover it are the antarāya, just mentioned, the knowledge obscuring (jnānāvaraniya), the darshana obscuring (darshanā varaniya), and the intoxicating or right belief preventing – (mohaniya). Those which do not cover up the spiritual nature of the soul, are the 3rd class (vedaniya karma), the 5th class (ayuh karma), the 7th class (gotra karma) and the 6th class (nāma karma). (These last two are out of order).

These karmas are forces, they are living forces, not forces such as gravity, steam, or electricity.

It is important to point out what has already been stated: namely that the combination of the soul with the karma is a very subtle combination which can only be reduced by mental and moral disciplines, hence the body is not in mechanical combination with the soul and cannot be separated and joined again like taking off and putting on a coat. The soul and the body stay in combination until death, and if the body is in bed the soul is there also.

Also the avadhi form of knowledge, by which the soul comes to know distant material things without the action of the sense organs or the mind, operates while the senses are awake, and is in addition to and not replacing the ordinary five senses. All the higher forms of knowing are in addition to the lower forms, the lower forms do not drop away as the higher ones develop; the five ways of knowing given are simply the order in which the soul developes itself. All knowledge is based on sensation.

And so we have in this rough classification of karmas, no

less than 158 energies which are in us either active or dormant ready to break out as soon as the circumstances allow or cause. They are given in continuation of a previous series of 12 lectures on mental concentration, and the idea is that the bad energies should be removed and good ones generated, or developed.

The quality of the soul which comes out upon the removal of the 7th class of karma, is that the circumstances or surroundings are neither high nor low; and when the 8th class is removed the quality of the soul that comes out is infinite capacities of activity. (Not omnipotence. Yet cannot create souls, in the sense of their not having previously existed).

List of the 158 Karmas

Class 1.	Jnānavaraniya karma	...	5 kinds
Class 2.	Darshanāvaraniya karma	...	9 kinds
Class 3.	Vedaniya karma	...	2 kinds
Class 4.	Mohaniya karma	...	28 kinds
Class 5.	Ayuh karma	...	4 kinds
Class 6.	Nāma karma	...	103 kinds
Class 7.	Gotra karma	...	2 kinds
Class 8.	Antarāya karma	...	5 kinds
			158

This classification is from the point of view of the nature or function of the karma. It is not from the point of view of the generation of karma, or working out of karma.

Causes of Karmas

Four general causes of karma have already been given, namely delusion (mithyātva), avirati, kashāya, and yoga (it is easier to use these names than to use a whole sentence in English for each cause). But these causes are each subdivided in greater detail.

Mithyātva. There are five kinds of this cause, namely:

1. Abhigraha mithyātva. It is a state of mind in which you stick to a false belief. You may not know it. If you think, speak, or act when in this state, you generate fresh karma (the kinds of karma which are generated by these causes are given in the next series, of Stages of Development following).
2. Anabhigraha mithyātva. It is a state of mind in which a person thinks "well, this may be true, and also that may be true," or "All religions are true." He does not go into the matter.
3. Abhinivesha mithyātva. It is the state of intentionally sticking to a false opinion when it is known or believed to be a false one.
4. Samshaya mithyātva. It is the state of doubt as to whether a given course of action is right or wrong. You stand still.
5. Anābhoga mithyātva. It is a state of lack of development, and the entity, therefore sticks to a false belief or has no belief; not having developed the faculties of judgement, conviction, discretion, &c., he does not come to a conclusion.

These causes are only the instrumental or determinant causes of the generation of the karma, the substantial cause is the individual himself (of herself, of course always understood). The above mentioned particular states of the individual are determinant causes of the generation of karma; they are from the ideal standpoint unnatural states. In every effect there are two causes, the substantial and the instrumental, both equally necessary for the effect.

Avirati: It is the laxity or looseness either of thought or sense activities. There are the following 12 kinds;

1. Lack of control of the thoughts. In spite of knowing that we should not have, or in spite of our wish not to have evil thoughts about people, still we have them, such as thoughts of revenge, thoughts of cheating other people, of deceiving them, of hurting them, etc., and so we generate karmas.
2. Lack of control of the sense of touch.
3. Lack of control of the sense of taste.
4. Lack of control of the sense of smell.
5. Lack of control of the sense of sight.
6. Lack of control of the sense of hearing,
7. Lack of control of the mind or senses in regard to living beings not having the power of locomotion, and whose bodies are particles of earth–earth beings.
8. Lack of control of the mind or senses in regard to living beings not having the power of locomotion, and whose bodies are particles of water–water beings.
9. Lack of control of the mind or senses in regard to living beings not having the power of locomotion, and whose bodies are particles of air–air beings.
10. Lack of control of the mind or senses in regard to living beings not having the power of locomotion, and whose bodies are particles of fire–fire beings.
11. Lack of control of the mind or senses in relation to vegetables.
12. Lack of control of the mind or senses in relation to living beings that have the power of locomotion.

Kashāya, is moral uncleanness, and there are 25 states taken into consideration as being states which, when the person is in, become the cause of the generation of karma.

1 to 4 Four degrees of anger,

5 to 8 Four degrees of pride,

9 to 12 Four degrees of deceitfulness,

13 to 16 Four degrees of greed,

17 to 25 The same as the remaining mohaniya karmas, laughing and joking, etc, down to the neuter sex passion.

These are the same states as the 25 last mohaniya karmas, only here the point of view is that when in any one of these states, the person generates or adds to his present karma. If, however, the attitude of the mind is one of aloofness, then fresh karma is not generated, he does not then identify himself with the anger for instance, and so does not generate more.

Yoga: There are 15 kinds of this cause. In this relation in the Jain philosophy, the word yoga has the technical meaning of bodily, speech, or thought activity. (This is a technical meaning).

1. Satya-mano-yoga. Activity of the mind: it may be truthful: it generates a kind of karma.
2. Asatya-mano-yoga. Activity of the mind which implies falsehood.
3. Satyā-satya-mishrana-mano-yoga. A state of mind when you may be thinking of something and that of which you are thinking relates partly to truth and partly to something that is false. It is a mixture of the two previous kinds.
4. Asatya-mishrana-mano-yoga. Activity of the mind which has no reference to truth, does not relate to truth at all.

5–8. Four kinds of speech activity, namely the same as those of the thought activity only with regard to speech.

(In illustration of speech which does not relate to the subject of truth or falsity, the sentence: "Bring me my watch" is an example).

9–15. Seven kinds of bodily activity, namely: activity of the physical body, activity of the vaikriya body, activity of the āhāraka body, activity of the kārmana body. This last includes the taijassa, because these two bodies (the kārmana and the taijasa) stay with the soul until worked out; they go with the soul at death to the next state of life. Then there are three more, namely bodily activities which are mixtures of the karmana and taijassa with any few particles of either the audārika, vaikriya, or āhāraka body, before the body is fully formed. Mishra means compound. Audârika is the ordinary physical body.

That makes the causes 57 in number, classed under four heads of respectively 5 mithyātva, 12 avirati, 25 kashāya, and 15 yogas.

In removing these causes of the generation of karma, the mithyātva must be removed first; it is not possible to remove the avirati first, or the kashāya or the yoga. Then the next in order, is the avirati, which must be removed before the kashāya, and the last to be removed is the yoga. So that, in any person, where there is mithyātva there is also lack of control of the thought and senses, there is also the list of 25 kashāyas, either dormant or operating; and there are the 15 yogas.

STAGES OF DEVELOPMENT

This, now, is from the point of view of generating karmas, as distinguished from the point of view we have previously had of the nature of the karmas. The matter now is about the generation of karma.

In describing which causes generate any particular karma stages, are made use of as follows:

> There are 14 guna-sthāna or stages of development. Guna means virtue, development, the coming out of the real nature and essence of the soul. Sthāna means stage.
>
> These 14 may be roughly divided into 4 classifications (or five, see following), namely: (i. e. one for each cause).
>
> One in which all the four causes of karma work, i.e. the mithyātva, the avirati, the kashāya, and the yoga.
>
> Another in which only the last three determinant causes work, that is the avirati, the kashāya and the yoga.
>
> Another in which only the last two determinant causes work, that is the kashāya and the yoga.
>
> Another in which only the yoga works.

Then there is the 14th gunasthāna by itself. It lasts only for a few moments. There is neither the mithyātva, the avirati, the kashāya, nor the yoga working.

So that to work out the karmas, you begin with the mithyātva and remove it first.

It is important to remember always that, these 14 stages, now about to be described, are in their logical order and not in chronoligical order. In the morning, you may be in a low stage and in the afternoon in a higher one, or vice versa, you may be in a high stage in the morning and in a lower one in the afternoon. The point is that, while in such stages you develope such and such karmas, and while in a high one you develope only certain karmas – but all this comes in course.

Ist Stage of Development

Called the Mithyātva Gunasthāna. It is a state of the same as the first subdivision of the Class 4, or Mohaniya karma. It is a state in which the person has a very intense dislike of the truth, the dislike is so strong that he will not have anything to do with it at all. The karma has no intense as to prevent the possibility of believing the truth at all. It is the same as the above named (Class 4, subdivision No. 1) only the point of view now is different. The point of view, here, is the generation of fresh karma. There it was simply describing the characteristic or nature of the karma (of the activity).

In this Gunasthāna the living being is liable to generate any of the following karmas, namely:

1. Any of the Jnanāvaraniya karmas, that is of 5 kinds.
2. Any of the Darshanāvaraniya karmas, that is of 9 kinds.
3. Either of the two Vedaniya karmas, that is of 2 kinds.
4. Any of the Mohaniya karmas, except, the sub-divisions Nos. 2 and 3, because these are never generated, they are simply milder forms of the activity of the subdivision No. 1 (called mithyātva mohaniya karma). We generate the mithyātva mohaniya and in its working out it may manifest as subdivision 2 or subdivision 3 (called respectively mishra mohaniya karma and samyaktva mohaniya karma). That makes 26 kinds liable to be generated.
5. Either of the 4 ayuh karmas, namely 4 kinds.
6. Any, out of 64 of the nāma karmas. (For this purpose of considering the generation of the karmas, the 103 nāma karmas are considered as 67, by including the 15 kinds of Bandhana nāma karma and the 5 kinds of samghatana in the 5 sharira; and then the colour, the smell, the taste, and the touch nāma karmas are each considered as being only one kind, disregarding their various subdivisions, thus making only 4 kinds instead of 20 kinds, or 16 fewer, which together with the above 20 makes in all 36 fewer than 103, or 67).

7. Either of the gotra karmas, that is of 2 kinds.
8. Either of the antarāya karmas, that is of 5 kinds.

In the first classification of the karmas, the total is 158. Reducing this by the above named 36, the remainder is 122. In the present mithyātva gunasthāna, the living being, therefore is liable to generate any one of 117 out of these 122 karmas. (It will, of course, be seen what this means. I say this myself only, but it follows that a man may generate an animal or insect or what not body).

So there are 5 karmas which are not generated in this mithyātva gunasthāna, and they are:

1. The Mishra mohaniya karma,
2. The samyaktva mohaniya karma,
3. The āhāraka sharira nāma karma,
4. The āhāraka Upānga nāma karma,
5. The Tirthankara nāma karma.

Then, there are certain karmas which are generated only in this stage and in no other, they are 16 in all:

1. Mithyātva mohaniya karma.
2. The neuter sex passion karma.
3. The naraka āyuh karma (This is important to notice).
4. The naraka gati nāma karma.
5. The jāti nāma karma, giving only one sense organ.
6. The jāti nāma karma, giving only two sense organ.
7. The jāti nāma karma, giving only three sense organ.
8. The jāti nāma karma, giving only four sense organ.
9. The chhevaththhu samhanana nāma karma (The living being would not even have sockets).
10. The hunda sansthāna nāma karma.
11. The naraka anupurvi nāma karma.

12. The ātāpa nāma karma.
13. The stāvara nāma karma (to stationary body).
14. Sukshma nāma karma (minute body).
15. The aparyāpta nāma karma (dies before completing the body).
16. Sādhārana nāma karma (common body).

So that, in order to avoid generating any of these 16 karmas, we must get away from the mithyātva state.

2nd Stage of Development

The above 16 karmas are not generated in this stage; of the 117 karmas generated (liable to be generated) in the first stage, the remaining 101 may also be generated in this stage.

In this stage, the 5 mithyātva causes do not work. They are controlled. It is to be remembered that 'causes' here means only the instrumental or determinant cause; the living being himself is always the real cause (or rather the substantial cause, both causes are equally necessary and real).

This stage is called 'sāsvadana' gunasthāna. It is only a momentary state. It is after anger, for instance, has risen and then subsided, and then is rising again; there is a momentary sensation of the taste of the quiet state; taste of the control of the mithyātva karma. It is not the state when the anger was subsided, that is a higher one, it is the momentary taste of that quiet state. It does not last long enough for the generation of some of the karmas.

The following 25 karmas liable to be generated in this stage, would not be generated in any higher stage:

1. Tiryancha gati nāma karma. In any higher stage than this 2nd stage, you do not generate a karma which takes you to the animal state.

2. Tiryanchāyuh karma.
3. Tiryanch anupurvi nāma karma.
4. Styānarddhi darshanāvaraniya karma (Somnambulistic).
5. Nidrā-nidrā (sleep requiring touching of the body to arouse the person).
6. Prachalā-prachalā (asleep while the body is walking).
7. Daurbhāgya nāma karma (unpopular).
8. Duhsvara nāma karma. (Unmusical voice).
9. Anādeya nāma karma (words do not carry weight).
10. The worst degree of anger (Mohaniya subdivision 4).
11. The worst degree of pride.
12. The worst degree of deceit.
13. The worst degree of greed.
14. The nyagrodha samsthāna nāma karma.
15. The sādi sansthāna nāma karma.
16. The Kubja sansthāna nāma karma.
17. The Vāmana sansthāna nāma karma.
18. The Rishabha-nārācha-samhanana nāma karma (bone joint).
19. The Nārācha-samhanana.
20. The Ardha-nārācha samhanana.
21. The Kilikā samhanana.
22. The Nicha gotra karma.
23. The Udyota nāma karma.
24. The Vihayo-gati nāma karma (bad gait).
25. The feminine sex passion.

In this 2nd gunasthāna there are 50 determinant causes operative; the 5 mithyātvas as already mentioned do not work, and then there is the āhāraka yoga and the āhāraka mishra yoga which do not operate.

(There seems to be a mistake about the hundā sansthāna nāma karma, it seems to me it ought to be generatable in this 2nd stage, seeing that the animal karmas can be generated, the tiryancha-gati, etc).

It may be useful here to mention four points of view with regard to karma, namely:

Bandha. Means the process of actually becoming identified with or tied to the karma.

Udaya. Means literally 'rising up' or 'coming up' that is to say, the actual showing of the activity of the karma and experiencing the actual result of the karma.

Udiranā. Is the process of bringing the karma into operation earlier than it would naturally come into operation.

Sattā. Is the state of the karma between the time when it is bound to the soul or absorbed by the soul and when it manifests. It is the dormant karma that is in us.

And it may also be useful here to mention three states with regard to the karma so far as the working of it out is concerned, namely:

Upashama. This word is a noun, and means control. The state of upashama karma, therefore, would be the state of the karma, when it is pressed down or controlled: controlled by the will just when it is felt to be rising.

Kshāya. This word literally means destruction. So that kashāya karma would be the total working out of the karma; karma when it is entirely removed.

Kshāyopashama. Part of the karma is controlled and part worked out.

3rd Stage of Development Called the Mishra-drishti-guna-sthān

It is of only a few moments duration. In the first stage or mithyātva gunasthāna, the state of mind is such that there is a positive dislike and repulsion of the truth; in the 2nd stage or sāsvādana gunasthāna, there is just the state of the control of the mithyātva (delusion); in this mishra–drishti gunasthāna, there is neither like nor dislike for the truth when it is presented to you: you just let the truth pass by without either liking it or disliking it. It is a sort of indifference, and there is no great wish or desire or energy put forth in this state of mind. This third stage is the result of the rise of the mishra mohaniya karma (2nd sub-division of class 4). The mishra mohaniya karma is the most noticeable sign or characteristic of this stage.

Causes operative

In this stage, there are 43 out of the 57 determinant causes operative. Those not operative are: the 5 mithyātvas; the worst degree of respectively anger, pride, deceitfulness, and greed; the āhāraka mishra yoga, the āhāraka yoga, the kārmana yoga, the audārika mishra yoga, and the vaikriya mishra yoga.

Karmas not generated

In this third stage, the 25 karmas mentioned as being generated in no higher stage than the 2nd, would not be generated in this third stage. The 16 karmas generated in only the mithyātva gunasthāna are not generated in this third. Nor are the āhāraka sharira, the āhāraka upānga, or the tirthankara. The Deva āyuh and the manushy āyuh karmas are not generated in this third stage. And the mishra mohaniya and samyaktva mohaniya are not generated. This counts up to 48 karmas not generated, leaving 74 which may be generated, as follows below.

Āyuh karma cannot be generated in this stage, because that strong wish which is the factor of the intelligence which generates āyuh karma is not strong enough in this third stage to generate the karma. The faculty of decision, the faculty through which we determine, is not strong or active here, in this weak indifferent state.

Karmas liable to be generated

In this stage, the living being is liable to generate any one of 74 karmas, namely:

5 or all of the jnānāvaraniya

6 of the darshanāvaraniya

2 or all of the vedaniya

19 of the mohaniya

36 of the nāma

1 gotra

5 or all of the antarāya

(It is not necessary to name the particular 36 nāma karmas, as they can be arrived at by anyone who wants to know them by a little trouble).

The other point, namely karmas not generated after this stage, does not apply, is not needed.

With reference to the state of karma just mentioned called upashama, anger should be suppressed, controlled or pressed down; controlled by the will just when it is felt to be rising. (I appreciate this as indicating the way to really not be angry or to really remove anger as distinguished from the merely pretending not to be angry – or any other vice than anger; it is much easier to pretend not to have the defect, whatever it is, and to persuade oneself that one does not want it and will try to remove it, than it is to really determine to suppress or control the wrong state).

(Incidentally the Jain idea of the parts of a tree may be put in here, as I have them in my notes, and it was talked about at the time. The parts of a tree are: fruit, flowers, bark, wood, roots, leaves and seed. I think if I mistake not, no I am sure, the idea is that these are separate living beings which in their joint activity or life make what is known as a tree; the tree is not only one living being, that is the idea. And those like the leaves, flowers, and fruit which cannot live in circumstances of winter cold and snow die. And of course it also follows from this that ordinary flowers should not be picked. It is only a matter of degree of civilisation and development whether a person feels gentle and careful and thoughtful to this, to us, rather great extent. Protection to life in all forms is the behaviour *natural* to a highly developed soul, as 1 understand it).

Before proceeding with the next gunasthāna, the 4th, there must be something said of what is called 'samyaktva'; it cannot be translated by one English word.

Samyaktva

As soon as the mithyātva (delusion) is controlled, or inoperative, then there comes out the contrary quality called samyaktva. The tva means ness.

The essential for the appearance of this state is that the worst degree of anger, of pride, of deceitfulness, and of greed are removed, or at least controlled and inoperative. Then a right attitude of thought, a right attitude towards truth, comes out. You are, for instance, convinced that to kill a living being is wrong. There is a relish of such convictions.

A man's whole progress depends upon his acquiring this samyaktva; and it is present in each of the remaining 11 gunasthāna or stages of development. It is, therefore, present in the next gunasthāna to be described, namely the 4th. All philosophy so-called and concentration, are of no use or are all false unless this state is reached. How, then, is this samyaktva to be reached ?

The man who wishes to obtain samyaktva must pass through three stages or processes. They are called respectively: yathā-pravritti-karana, apurva-karana, and ani-vritti-karana. But before describing them something must be said about the duration of karmas and the Jain idea of time.

The first of these three processes lessens the duration of the karmas, and that is the first thing to do in order to obtain the samyaktva.

Time is the duration of the modifications of substances. Duration is the fact that a given state of anything or being stays for a certain length of time. The modification (or state, that is) lasts for a certain length of time. (Time is not, therefore, any mysterious mystery, it is quite plain and graspable).

The maximum time that the karmas could last is as follows; that is to say that any given karma which is in combination with the soul, would naturally be worked out during the time as given below; but then it is to be understood that while this particular karma is working out, the individual may generate an addition of karma of a similar nature, and so although at the end of the following maximum times, the particular karma, would all be rid from the soul, yet the soul would be in combination with fresh karma if the inflow has not been stopped.

Maximum durations of the karmas

The maximum duration of a jnānāvaraniya karma could not be more than 3,000,000,000,000,000 sāgaropamas; of a darshanāvaraniya karma the same; of a vedaniya karma the same; of a mohaniya karma 7,000,000,000,000,000 sāgaropamas; of a nāma karma 2,000,000,000,000,000 sāgaropamas; of a gotra karma the same; of an antarāya karma 3,000,000,000,000,000 sāgaropamas.

This subject is being considered with a view to showing how the samyaktva can be reached; and so far as the samyaktva is concerned the āyuh karma is necessary and is not taken into account.

A sâgaropama is one thousand billion (that is to say in figures 1,000,000,000,000,000) palyopamas.

A palyopama is an innumerable (not infinite, but having a limit) quantity of years, so great that it cannot be numbered. An innumerable quantity is a limited quantity and will in time be exhausted. An infinite quantity will never be exhausted.

Although the above numbers are immense, still, in view of the theory that so far as the past is concerned, we have not been without karma, the duration of our various karmas has already been considerably more than the above mentioned numbers of years.

In the Jain idea of time the smallest division is called a 'samaya'. In a wink of the eye, for instance, and such similar durations, there are innumerable samayas.

Innumerable samayas would make one âvali.

16, 777, 216 âvalis make one muhurta (equal to 48 minutes, English time).

30 Muhurtas would make one day.

15 Days would make 1fortnight, etc.

Innumerable years, as already mentioned, make one palyopama.

To illustrate to the mind, the idea of a palyopama, if you dig a hole in the ground 8 miles long, 8 miles wide, and 8 miles deep, fill it with hair cut up into the shortest possible lengths, and press it into the whole, by marching heavy processions, steam rollers, or anything similar, over it, and then once a year, take out a piece of the hair, it will in time become emptied, but it will be in an innumerable quantity of years.

Come back, now, to the processes through which one must

pass, in order to reach the state of samyaktva. The first thing to do is to lesson the duration of the karmas, and the amount by which the duration is to be lessened, is the next question. Each of the seven above named karmas must be reduced to 100,000,000 000,000 years maximum duration; and when the living being experiences the feeling, that this whole embodied life is a misery, it shows that this work of reduction has been done. This is the first process, called yathâ-pravritti-karana. This is only possible for a five-sense-organ mind endowed living being. Other lower living beings do not pass through this experience or first process at all. But this experience may be felt infinity of times and still the living being may not pass into the next or second process.

2nd Process

A muhurta, as already mentioned, is 48 minutes English time, and 30 muhurtas are therefore, one day. If the living being can succeed in reducing by only 48 minutes, this one hundred billion years maximum duration of the karmas, he is then in the 2nd process, called apurva-karana which has to be passed through in order to obtain the samyaktva condition. This second process consists in the manifestation of a desire to remove the worst degree of anger, of pride, of deceitfulness, and of greed. The first time this desire is experienced shows that this further reduction in the maximum duration has been effected. The literal meaning is 'not previously'; that is, this desire has not been previously experienced.

3rd Process

The third process is the actual control of the worst degree of anger, of pride, or deceitfulness, and of greed. Deceit is the conflict between the thought and the action, as already mentioned. The worst degree of anger is that which lasts the whole life time, and the way to test ourselves as to whether we have reached the 2nd process (apurva-karana) is by considering and seeing whether there is any person, we know towards whom we are chronically angry; and then the thought that we ought not after all to be so, would show that we were in the second process. The 3rd process is the actual control of the worst anger, pride, deceitfulness, and greed. The end of the apurva-karana is the beginning of the ani-vritti-karana.

When these three processes have been passed through, then the 'knot' is cut, so to speak, and the lowest kind of samyaktva is reached. The 'knot' is the attack upon us of our inborn likes and dislikes, more especially as to convictions regarding conduct, (that it is wrong to kill, etc). When these three processes have been passed through, then, the three darshana mohaniya karmas and the four worst degrees, just mentioned, are controlled or inoperative.

The worst degree of the four degrees which were mentioned of anger, pride, deceitfulness, and greed, is called the 'anantânubandhi' degree. 'An' means no, 'ant' means end, 'ânubandhi' means bound as cause and effect. The whole word means 'life long effect'. Anantânubandhi anger is that anger which lasts the whole life time.

When the samyaktva is reached or appears, mithyātva or delusion is controlled.

Mithyātva (or delusion, or false belief, or false conviction regarding conduct, e.g., that it would be right to kill) is of several kinds, but can be divided into two, namely:

1. Avyakta or indefinite mithyātva.
2. Vyakta, or definite mithyātva.

There is a class of living beings, with which the universe is packed, so that there is not an inch of space, anywhere, and these are not. These living beings are conscious, they are very minute, and cannot be seen with eye or microscope, fire will not kill them, nor will water, they pass through these things without being hurt, no human instrument can kill these living beings, they can pass through mountains–anything. There are an infinity of these living beings and this is the source whence come the developing and liberated souls. They have an indefinite existence. They are called 'nigoda'.

Development Begins

The mithyātva of these nigoda is avyakta mithyātva or indefinite; it has not taken any shape, whereas, the mithyātva of human beings is shaped and definite. A person has certain views on certain subjects.

The mithyātva in the mithyātva gunasthāna of first stage of development is the definite kind; the indefinite kind is not a stage of development and the nigoda are in that indefinite state of existence, which is the state of existence before development has begun.

When, once, out of the indefinite mithyātva state, the living being never goes back to it; if it goes back to the nigoda state it goes back as a nigoda of a different kind, namely, having vyakta or definite mithyātva. There are therefore two kinds of nigoda, one with indefinite mithyātva whose development has not begun, and the other kind with definite mithyātva whose development begun and who are therefore in the first stage of development, or mithyātva gunasthāna.

The answer to the very natural question which arises here, "What starts the development?" would be something like this: in a whirlpool some bit of stick or paper or other matter may in the surging of the water get to one side and become separated from the rest, be caught by the wind, and dried by the sun; and so some such thing may happen to a nigoda which would awaken just a spark of the latent potential power of development.

It is also the theory of the Jinas that as a soul passes from the embodied to the liberated state, a nigoda comes out and begins development. But this does not mean that a nigoda comes out only on such occasions.

There are, according to the Jain philosophy, three kinds of living beings, namely;

1. Those whose nature it is to remain in the embodied state. They may be men, animals, or other living beings: they are content to remain embodied and never wish for nor reach the liberated state.
2. There are living beings whose nature it is to reach liberation.
3. And there are living beings whose nature it is to reach liberation, but they do not do so, because they do not get the right or necessary circumstances.

It is understood that these and the first kind are very few in number, and it is no misery to them to remain in the embodied state.

The approximate English translation of the words in the chart given is as follows:

Sansâri (adjective), means those living beings who are in an embodied state.

Siddha (all these words are adjectives modifying living being). This word means those who have reached the liberated state.

Sayogi, those embodied ones who have not stopped the activities of body mind, and speech.

Ayogi, those who have done so. (This is only a momentary state just before passing to liberation).

Chhadmastha, living beings with imperfect knowledge.

Kevali, living beings with perfect knowledge, omniscience.

Samohi, those who still have the intoxicating elements (that is the mohaniya karmas or the kashâyas).

Amohi, those whose moha has disappeared.

Udita-mohi, those in whom the moha (intoxicating elements) is actually seen, working, manifesting.

Anudita-mohi, those in whom it is under control, checked, or at the bottom, like mud in a clear brook.

Bâdara-mohi, those who recognize only rough kinds or gross subdivisions of their moha, such as anger, pride, deceitfulness, greed, etc.

Sukshma-mohi, those who recognize delicate or subtle subdivisions, such as more and less intense degrees of anger etc.

Shreni-rahita, rahita means without. Those who are without any system of working out their moha (delusion).

Shreni-vanta, those who have a method by which they systematically work out their infatuating or intoxicating or delusion, producing elements.

Avirati, those who have not yet obtained control over their minds and senses.

Virati, those who have obtained a partial control over their mind and senses.

Mithyātvi, those who are in the state of mithyātva.

Samyaktvi, those who are in the state of samyaktva.

Granthi-abhedi, those who have not yet cut that 'knot' spoken of previously (this knot is cut while in the state of mithyātva).

Granthi-bhedi, those who have cut it.

Abhavya, those who will not reach liberation.

Bhavya, those who will reach it.

The following is another division of living beings. It is a division by dichotomy.

Souls

- Sansāri — Siddha
- Sayogi — Ayogi
- Chhadmastha — Kevali
- Samohi — Amohi
- Udit-mohi — Anudit-mohi
- Bādar-mohi — Sukshma mohi
- Shreni-rahita — Shreni-vanta
- Avirati — Virati
- Mithyātvi — Samyaktvi
- Granthi-abhedi — Granthi-bhedi
- Abhavya — Bhavya

This table is read upwards, thus: there are abhavya living beings and bhavya living beings, but they are both granthi-abhedi; there are granthi-abhedi living beings and granthi-bhedi living beings, but they are both mithyātvi; there are mithyātvi living beings and samyaktvi living beings, but they are both avirati, and so on up to the top. There are sansāri living beings and siddha living beings, but they are both living beings.

As already mentioned all progress depends upon samyaktva, samyaktva having been described as the control of the three darshana mohaniya karmas and the four anantānubandhis. Concentration and philosophy proper cannot be exercised until this state called samyaktva is obtained.

Signs of Samyaktva

If you are in the state of samyaktva then you will have certain very definite convictions, concerning three principles, namely concerning the principle of the Deity, the principle of the Teacher (Guru), and the principle of Dharma (right life, duty).

The Deity

The Deity, as understood in this system of philosophy, is the highest ideal that we keep before the mind, and with the object that we may ultimately become like him. It does not mean a Deity who issues laws that must be obeyed, or a creator of the universe. One must have an ideal, an ideal manhood, that he wishes to attain to; and if not to be attained in the body as the Master was, still to reach the liberated state where all persons are in a state of equality. The attaining to this ideal will be the aim and end of all the actions during life, and so if we get a wrong ideal man, then in trying to become so we lead wrong lives. The ideal man should be called the Deity (Deva). The Deity (Deva) is a person living as a human being in the midst of his brothers and sisters, not his children. There are millions of Devas (The Tirthankara is the Master) who were such men, being now in the liberated state (and once liberated the Deity is never again embodied, the soul after reaching perfection never again becomes imperfect, and an embodied state is an imperfect one).

Now, what is the difference between the Deva or Arhat as understood in this system of philosophy and the Deity as understood in other systems, Krishna, Buddha, Christ, etc, etc.?

If you find the following 18 characteristics in him, then he is a Deva. Try to test all the so-called Deities as to whether they have these 18 characteristics, and then if any is found wanting reject the Deities so-called: that is the Jain teaching. If any one of the following 18 characteristics is missing then he is not a Deva:

1-5. The antarāya karmas must all have disappeared in him, because so long as there is any antarāya karma in a person, that shows that, that person may be willing to do a right thing and still is not able to do it, it shows that in his nature there is still some kind of weakness; therefore he cannot be an ideal of perfection. There are 5 antaraya karmas, and so that makes the first 5 characteristics.

6. Laughing and joking must have disappeared; because when some unfamiliar object will produce laughing, it shows a lack of knowledge, and that shows that the jnānāvaraniya karmas are not fully worked out; but in the Deva or Arhat it is fully worked out and therefore there is nothing unfamiliar to him. If laughing is produced by some new peculiar relationship of ideas, it would show a lack of knowledge.

7. He has no liking for this, that, and the other thing; that is, for material objects; he might say "You can keep them". It makes the person an unhappy person when he likes a thing and has to go without it.

8. He has no positive dislike for anything, because dislike is also the cause of misery.

9. He is not afraid of anything. Fear has disappeared from him. Weakness and lack of knowledge cause fear. There is fear for the loss of one's body, there is fear for the loss of one's reputation, property, fame, popularity etc. only when these are identified with the self; and such fear shows that the person considers these things,

property, reputation, embodied life, etc., to be the factors of his being; he has not realised that his real self is different from these things, his goods, his emotions, his physical body, his reputation, etc. and that his real self cannot be injured by any of these losses. Fear for the loss of these things implies that he thinks that those things are the factors of his being (whereas they are not, he can live independently of them) that they are his self, and that if they are destroyed, he is destroyed with them. An Arhat would not have fear with regard to anything. Fear shows lack of knowledge and weakness.

Here was given a train of reasoning by which we may know that the soul must and does exist: Matter is indestructable. If the state called knowledge can be proved to be different (which of course it can) from motion of matter, not only in degree but in kind; as the attributes of black etc., are attributes of objects, so the attribute of 'knowing' and the attribute of morality or mode of behaviour must be the attributes of some real thing – call it soul, self, ego, individual, or what not. And as matter cannot be destroyed, so this soul cannot be destroyed. And it is not a compound; it is a unit always itself. It must exist for ever. That it will exist always in some state or other is the essential of a reality. It is one of the natures of a reality to exist.

10. He has no feeling of disgust or sense of repulsion. The reason would be that the sense of disgust produces a kind of misery; and in the ideal man there must be no misery; also there is no sense of disgust when it is known that the object of disgust could only exist in those conditions: if there is disgust it is because only one or two of the aspects of the object are considered; if all the aspects are known then there is not any disgust: and so if there is any sense of disgust it shows

lack of knowledge, and in the Arhat or Deva, or Deity there must be no lack of knowledge.

11. You do not find sorrow. Sorrow is a misery. He may have compassion.
12. Sexual passion or lust has disappeared entirely; because in that state a person will do all kinds of wrong things to gratify the passion.
13. His attitude of belief and convictions is correct; he is not in any state of intoxication or delusion. All signs of greed, anger, killing etc. must have gone. He has dismissed mithyātva.
14. Ignorance has gone, and therefore he is Omniscient.
15. He never goes into the state of sleep. If there is any hitch in the continuity of his omniscience then he is not an Arhat.
16. He has a perfect control over his desires; over any desire to please the eye, or the taste, or the ear, or the sense of touch.
17. He has no attachments to things or persons. He would never say "You cannot take it, it is mine". (This characteristic refers more to persons, while the 7th refers more to things).
18. He has no hatreds of persons or things. He does not think "I do not want anything to do with that person".

The person who has obtained the samyaktva has the conviction that such a person and such a person alone is my God, in the sense of an ideal man (not as creator), and this is a strong conviction of which he is quite sure without any wavering. The samyaktva spoken of so far is called Upashamika samyaktva. The upashamika means that the karmas mithyātva mohaniya and the four anantānubandhis are controlled (not removed).

The Teacher

The person who has obtained the samyaktva would have certain convictions regarding what sort of a man could be his teacher. He would have the conviction that the only kind of person who can teach the truth in the absence of the Deva or Arhat is one who has the below mentioned characteristics. Unless a person has the following qualifications he cannot be the right kind of teacher, able to teach us the truth:

1. He does not destroy any form of life, animal, vegetable, or mineral (water, for instance) through carelessness of body, mind, and speech. It is, therefore impossible for him to be a layman.
2. His speech is actually truth in fact, and is spoken in a pleasant way, and is spoken only when the teacher (guru) thinks that it is beneficial to the person to whom it is spoken.
3. He does not take anything which is not given to him by its owner. And he only takes those things which are necessary for the maintenance of the body. That is a general statement. Now we have a more detailed one. Things which are given to him by the owner and which he accepts may be either;

   (i) **Inanimate**. He does not accept any inanimate thing that is not given to him by its owner, such as books, clothes, needles, cotton, drugs, etc. etc.

   (ii) **Animate**. He would not accept an animate object even if the owner offers it, such as a bird, or a dog. In the case of animate objects, it is true that the owner may be willing to give or part with it, but then "Is the animal willing to give his body over to me?" would be the question that would arise, and if the animal were willing, still it would not be right, the animal would be insane. Therefore the teacher does not accept animate objects even if offered by the owner.

(iii) If anything is made specially for the teacher, such as an article of food, he will not accept it.

(iv) While a thing may not have been specially prepared for the teacher (guru), still if that guru's guru thinks that he ought not to have some special thing, then if the layman offers that thing to the young guru, it ought not to be accepted. This much of obedience is prescribed by the Jain philosophy. He does not, however, obey everything implicitly, for instance, he would not obey if told to kill. The reason we will not accept food that has been specially prepared for him is that, by doing so he shares in the karma of producing the article. He always goes unexpectedly to the house.

4. He has entirely given up the sex passion. This is the fourth characteristic which the teacher must have in order to be able to tell us the truth.
5. He does not own any property that is in the sense of ownership as understood in law. His clothing is given to him but he does not have them as 'owning' them. He only holds them as custodian; books, etc.

The guru may be a man or a woman.

If a person does not have all the above characteristics, the person who has obtained the samyaktva, is convinced that he cannot be the right kind of teacher able to teach us the truth; – if he uses all sorts of false politeness he is not a man able to teach the truth.

Dharma

Dharma means the body of rules of conduct. It does two things, it prevents a living being from falling down spiritually, and it helps him to go up spiritually. These rules apply to all living beings, not only to man. All living beings are social, and these rules have something to do with a living being's relationships with other living beings. Our own development only takes place by reason of our actions and life in relation to other living beings. The ultimate object of all these rules so far as they are social, must come to this: that we must do some good to our fellow beings. The object is that we may be able to do some good to the people around us. The basis of these rules is pity, compassion, love, doing good, benevolence, kindness, etc. (called dayā).

'Dayā' can be manifested in many ways, and we want to know them, dayā being the foundation of the rules.

One of the ways in which dayā would be shown, would be that he would follow the good ways of his family, for instance, in not killing flies, etc. This is called dravya dayā – the right action without knowing why, that is to say, when the internal attitude of mind is not active.

A second way in which dayā would manifest itself, would be that we should feel a desire that other living beings should develop their *spiritual* nature; the previous way mentioned simply protected the *bodily* welfare. Here the desire is to do good to the soul of the other living being. This form is called bhāva dayā.

Sva dayā. A third way in which dayā shows itself. Sva means 'one's own'. It is a feeling of pity for the soul that it should have been so long, that is for all past time, in the deluded state of mithyātva – this pity comes after the samyaktva has been experienced: and in consequence of this feeling of pity, he takes care to remain aloof, from the pains and pleasures of life letting them come and go without indentifying his own self with them. He gets to know that these bodily pains and pleasures are enemies to an obscure the bliss quality of the real self.

Para dayā. Para means others. This is a love for others; but the difference between this and the dravya dayā is that, the para dayā is the result of thought, whereas you were simply born into the dravya dayā and followed it blindly. Here the thought is: "I do not like pain or misery, therefore other people or other living beings, animals, birds, etc, would not; and therefore I shall endeavour to avoid inflicting any pain or misery upon them".

Svarupa dayā. Is a refraining from injuring other living beings because you wish to obtain a pleasurable condition, such as that of the devas (not Deity, but the beings in the pleasurable devā state). You believe that by not killing or hurting, you will reach a pleasurable condition, and for that reason, you do not kill or hurt. This is good, but not the highest dayā.

Anubandhi dayā. Literally means dayā in the result and not in the beginning. It is, for instance, telling anyone something unpleasant, in order that, they may come to their senses, but there is no vindictiveness or anger in this anubandhi dayā; if the correction arises from anger, it is not dayā. The real desire here, is to benefit the other person. If there is any feeling of revenge or hate then it is not dayā.

That makes six ways in which dayā shows itself.

The person in the state of samyaktva is convinced that only a body of rules which is based on dayā is true dharma or true conduct rules, true religion, or the right law of life, and that no other body of rules, such as one that is based on killing animals for sacrifices, can be a right one. And it is a strong conviction, about which there is no wavering.

After reaching this state of conviction with regard to the Deity, the Master, and Dharma, a person may feel doubtful or unsteady on the subject; not so as to destroy the virtue of samyaktva, but to soil it, so to speak. It may be compared to injuring the body and not killing it. The things which soil the samyaktva are called atichāras, and the following five are given:

1. **Shankā**, means doubt. This would be the first transgression of samyaktva. You may doubt the truth of some of the statements of the philosophy; but this doubt is that which comes after having once been convinced of the truth of the statement. The doubt called samshaya mithyatva (under causes) is a doubt experienced before ever having experienced the conviction of the truth of a statement.

   When a statement is heard or read (this refers of course more particularly to philosophical and religious matters) instead of saying "It may or may not be true" the fact should be recognised that the inability to understand the statement, is due to weakness, which will in time disappear.

2. **Ākānkshā**. It is the state of mind which argues that because a person can do wonderful things or so-called miraculous things that therefore such person can make true statements, with regard to truth and life and the universe. The fact is that, rogues and rascals are able to do wonderful things just as can good men. If a man were able, for instance, by speaking a word to reduce a teaspoon to powder, and then said "In the same way I can reduce a house to powder", that would be all right. But the fact that the man can do this, is no proof that he can make true statements with regard to truth.

3. **Vitigichchhā**. This is the third mode of wavering from samyaktva. It is when after having followed the religion for a length of time, and then illness, or suffering, or losses, or disasters come upon you, you blame the philosophy and doubt its efficiency. The truth of the

philosophy must not be blamed, but the cause of the suffering should be looked for, in past actions.

4. **Mithyātva-prashansā**. Literally means praise of any one, who is in mithyātva. The feeling that the fakirs, who do all manner of absurd things must be very wonderful people with a truer religion; also the admiration of abominable person, who can be proved to be following wrong lives, Napoleon, Armour, Butchers, etc.

5. **Atiparichaya**. Literally means too much familiarity. It means the feeling towards a bosom friend that you can not do without him (or her) &c., must always be with him, etc. It causes you to get into his way of life and so you soil your samyaktva.

When a person is convinced as above described regarding the Deity, the Teacher, and the Dharma he naturally makes a vow that he will not fall into these transgressions or waverings from such convictions.

Also it follows that, anyone having these convictions will test and criticise any person claiming to be a Deity, or a Teacher, and if any of the 18 or the 5 characteristics, above mentioned, are found wanting, he will reject such person as not being fully to be relied upon. This applies also to the clergy and other persons claiming to be spiritual teachers.

It is stated that the last Arhat, whose name was Mahāvira, and whom history describes, possessed the 18 characteristics mentioned. It is in the history of the Jain people that this is to be found.

All the liberated or perfected living beings have become so, by reason of their own efforts, in an evolution from the nigoda state.

The following are five signs or characteristics of samyaktva, and from them, we may know by our own inner thoughts what our attitude is, towards the universe in which we find ourselves, and whether or not we are in the state of samyaktva. They are internal signs, so that each can test himself.

1. **Upashama**, is a mental state when the strong intoxicating karmas or the kashāyas like anger, greed, etc.; are suppressed or controlled. And the suppression has taken place either naturally, because the karma is exhausted, or else by thinking on the matter and realizing that after all, by being engrossed in the worst anger, greed, etc. we fall to such a depth that it takes a long time to come up again. If the suppression comes naturally, it is because the person has done the work before.
2. **Samvega** (noun), is a desire to reach the state of liberation.
3. **Nirveda**, is a recognition that this continual going on from incarnation to incarnation is not the right state of life; you look upon this or any embodied state as a misery and one to get away from. There is always the pain of birth and death.
4. **Anukampā**, is compassion for those who suffering from any kind misery. If the misery is due to their own ignorance and foolishness, then there is still pity for them that they should be thus ignorant. It is the duty of society to lesson the extent of suffering which exists among them.
5. **Āstikya**, is the conviction that, that only is the true dharma that has been taught by the Arhats, or persons in whom the 18 above named failings are absent. The conviction that only such a person can give a code of rules of life.

Dravya – Bhāva
Vyavahāra – Nishchaya

These two pairs of terms, which are terms of relationship, the first implying the thought about the other, will be required later on, and their meaning is therefore given now, as follows:

Dravya means literally the material out of which a thing is made. For instance, clay which was going to be made into a teacup, would be correctly called a dravya teacup. Mr. Smith, of London, if in his next incarnation, were going to be a butcher, would be correctly called a dravya butcher. Krishna, who is to be one of the future Arhats, might have been correctly called a dravya Arhat, while he was alive on earth. The previous state of the actual state is the dravya state. It always precedes the actual state in time.

Bhāva, the actual teacup would be the bhāva teacup, the actual butcher would be the bhāva butcher, the actual Arhat would be the bhāva arhat. The actual state is the bhāva state; the state going on, visible. It always comes after the dravya state.

Vyavahāra, is related to the word nishchaya. Vyavahāra prefixed to any state means the visible signs that you see. And it is necessary as illustration. Vyavahāra dharma, for instance, is the visible conduct of the man. It impresses upon the minds of people who see it the truth of the conduct. The description, which a man makes either for himself or to other people, of his Deva, of his Teacher, or of his rules of conduct, would be the vyavahāra deva, vyavahāra guru, vyavahāra dharma. Such description of devaship is like the peg on which, on account of weakness, the thoughts must be hung. Vyavahāra leads to nishchaya. But still it does not necessarily precede in time the nishchaya.

Nishchaya, is the term related to vyavahāra. It is the real internal state, that ought to accompany the vyavahāra acts. For instance, the nishchaya deva would be the internal condition or the *realisation* of the conviction that, there is in me the potentiality of becoming the Deva, I have described.

Vyavahāra Dharma, applying these two terms, vyavahāra and nishchaya, dharma is to be defined from these two points of view. Vyavahāra dharma is the action in accordance with the rules prescribed or taught by Arhats and accompanied always by days or based always upon dayā, which is a fellow feeling for other living beings; and vyavahāra dharma in order to be vyavahāra dharma must become the cause of nishchaya dharma. The love, compassion, sympathy, pity, etc. must accompany the practice of the rules, otherwise the practice is mere hypocrisy.

Nishchaya dharma would be the purity of the soul which results from the above mentioned pure action, and the sign of this purity of the soul is that the dirt of karma disappears (karma is a foreign element in combination with the soul). And the fruit of this purity of soul is samyaktva and other higher stages up to liberation. This purity of soul comes out from the action, from the vyavahāra dharma.

Dharma is not a something separate from the man. The rule is the man's idea, and the idea is part of or an aspect of the man. Dharma is nothing apart from the man; it is the state or action (state of knowledge, mode of behaviour) of the man.

Classification of Dharma

Dharma can first be divided into (1) the layman's, and (2) the monk's.

Leaving the dharma of the monk, the dharma of the layman can be divided into (a) ordinary or common dharma, and (b) special dharma.

We are in the course of dealing with the guna-sthānas or stages of development, in reference to which causes produce which karmas, and the third guna-sthāna has been described. This ordinary or common dharma comes in here now as a sort of digression, but it serves the purpose of showing how the man who wishes gets or helps himself to get the samyaktva, the samyaktva being in all the guna-sthāna or stages of development after the third guna-sthāna. So that these rules are as it were a link between the 3rd and 4th guna-sthāna.

Common Dharma

The ordinary or common dharma is the first step which a person desiring to make some spiritual progress should adopt. It is the way to commence working out the karmas, particularly the anger, pride, deceitfulness, and greed. The following 35 rules are the ordinary or common dharma.

1. The person who wishes to make some spiritual progress should follow some kind of business, trade, or profession, which is not of an ignoble or degrading nature; he should follow it in a just and fair way, and in proportion to his capital.

   This would include service in the employment of other people, and then in proportion to the capital would mean not undertaking to do more work than you have energy and strength to perform.

   All these rules are, as before said, based on dayā, i. e., doing good to and not causing injury to other living beings. Therefore the business must not be that of a butcher, brewer, (in fermentation there is infinite destruction of life), wine merchant, gun maker, or any business which involves or necessitates the wholesale destruction of life, whether animal or man, fish, bird, or insect.

   The reason why it is necessary for such a layman to undertake some business (a layman who wishes to make spiritual progress) is because by so doing he can provide himself with means;

(a) to maintain himself and anyone dependent upon him, and with means;

(b) to help those who are in distress. A layman cannot help much by teaching, that is to say spiritual help. By helping people in distress he removes bad karmas and generates good ones.

(c) Also with means to perform his dharma without too much difficulty and obstacle.

The reasons why he should do his business or profession in a fair and just way are because it is only money earned in a fair way that can be beneficial. If earned unfairly or dishonestly, then, while enjoying it or using it, there is all the time a kind of fear controlling the mind, lest the dishonesty be discovered. There is a consciousness of risk, or danger, not only from the police and government, but also from the general public. And when the money is earned in lair and honest ways, the mind remains in a peaceful state, and the wealth is therefore enjoyed and the religious functions are performed in a fearless way. That is all so far as the present life is concerned. Then so far as the future life is concerned you improve it by the association of virtuous people, which you cannot get if you earn money dishonestly; they will not come into contact with you. When acquiring money in a foul way the mind is in a foul state and you are generating bad karmas for the future.

These rules are for the beginner; if you wish to paint a photograph and the canvas is soiled, you must first clean it; these rules are as it were the cleaning process.

2. The layman should marry, with a person not of the same family or from the same ancestors; and whose

character, taste, culture, actions, language, etc., are of the same kind.

The idea here is that as the layman has not reached a stage of development where he can control his sex passion, marriage is better than promiscuous indulgence. He should not marry if he can control the sex passion. The reason for having a marriage partner of the same culture etc., is to render misunderstandings and discord or inharmony less liable than otherwise.

3. The lay person should always be cautious of danger spots (a) visible and (b) invisible.

   (a) Pursuits or pastimes the bad results of which are seen all around us, such as crime, which, we know, takes one to prison &c., lustfully eyeing other men's wives; gambling, etc.

   (b) Meat eating, drink, and any pursuit leading to bad results which can be known from thinking and reasoning.

   Of these dangerous pursuits a person should be wary, and even afraid.

4. The person who wishes to advance in spiritual progress should appreciate the conduct, life and doings of truly experienced persons. He may not be able to act as they do, but he can *appreciate* the actions.

   By experienced persons is meant persons who are experienced by reason of having come in contact with the wise. They would always try to do good to people who need to be done good to: they would always be grateful for kindness. They would even give up their own less important business, to do some more important thing for others. They would never malign, slander, or libel. They do not grieve at losses, or get elated at prosperity. They do not use too many words.

They do not make enemies through recklessness. They would always fulfill their promises. Such experienced people are called Shishta.

5. Is with regard to the degree that the sense pleasures should be enjoyed and controlled. The man having been for all time in the past enjoying the pleasures of the senses cannot at once give them up, and therefore some only need to be given up at first; and so he may enjoy sense pleasures to a degree commensurate with his business and house-hold duties, that is to say he should give up those sense pleasures which conflict with his duties. And he should control all those sense enjoyments which would encourage or feed any of the following six things, namely:

   (a) **Kāma** or sexual passion, lust, the lustful eye, in regard to a woman or girl not the man's own wife. This passion in this form should be conquered.

   (b) **Krodha** must be conquered. It is that emotion which is the cause of hurting or injuring done in a rash way. This may be called 'anger': there are the two elements of (i) injury to another, and (ii) rashness of the action or speech.

   (c) **Lobha** (greed) must be conquered; it is either or both of the following two modes of being greedy: (i) not relieving a genuine case of distress when you are appealed to or that comes to your notice, you, of course, being able to give the relief, (ii) taking property from people in an illegitimate way without any cause or reason: not by force but by persuasively getting the person to part with his property. Shop people do this when they induce to purchasers to buy goods. In theft this consent of the owner is not obtained, in theft the money is taken against the owner's will.

(d) **Māna** (pride) here has a special meaning; it means the non-acceptance of the teachings of persors who are actively engaged in attaining the state of liberation, and this non-acceptance comes on account of obstinacy. You think "I know just as well as he does" and you reject the teaching, without testing or examining it.

(e) **Mada**. This is pride or boasting about one's family, ancestors, etc., about one's strength or physical power; about one's greatness (a Lord might think himself a great person); about one's beauty or handsomeness, or about one's learning. This pride is liable to become the cause of hurting others if it makes him look down upon others and think that, being a superior being, he has the right to tyrannize.

(f) **Harsha**, literally means pleasure, but here it means in a technical sense giving pleasure to the mind by causing unnecessary pain to others, or by engaging in gambling, hunting, shooting, etc – sport.

Incidental: Insentient things are only temporarily units; but sentient beings remain the same individual for all time. Any insentient thing, as a teacup, consists of matter, and that matter did and always will exist in some relationship; it cannot be destroyed. A sentient being is a soul and cannot be destroyed as an individual.

6. The layman who wishes to take the first steps towards spiritual progress should avoid (or abandon) place of difficulties and dangers. For instance, a place of battle, or where plague, or famine is. Or where there is ill feeling towards him from the people around him (this is for the beginner). The reason is that if he stays in such places he will not be able to accomplish what he wishes to accomplish.

7. He should live in a State or Country where he will have adequate protection of his life and property from the rulers. If he lives where crimes go on unpunished he is liable to be disturbed.

8. The lay man should get the company of gentle people who appreciate good, whose actions are right, whose conduct is of the right kind, and who are always partial for virtue; and whom he considers as examples to be followed.

9. With regard to the home or house he wishes to establish, if any. There should not be bones underneath: the spot where it is built should not be too open or too much concealed. (This applied more especially to India in the past). The house should not be among quarrelsome, undesirable neighbours.

10. He should dress according to his means; should not spend beyond his means on dress; and if he has the means to dress extravagantly still he should not do so; that dress should not be too showy.

11. His expenses should be in proportion to his income.

12. When he lives in any country, if there is any particular, well known, established custom which does not involve the breaking of any high principle, such custom should be followed.

13. He should not get into any undesirable habits or practices, such as meat eating or wine drinking.

14. He should not label or slander anybody because this is done always with a view to harming the reputation of the person without any proper purpose. Showing up fraudulent people is not libel or slander, it is doing good. Do not libel or slander the King.

15-16. Keep the company of only pure hearted persons and

persons of good conduct; and do not keep the company of bad persons. The difference here from rule 8 is that this refers to equals; rule 8 refers to persons spiritually more advanced.

17. Respect the parents. The idea is that they have done so much for us that we should return something, we should return gratitude. If we cannot do this by giving them money we can do so by showing them the right path. Had they chosen not to care for us we should have suffered?

18. None of the person's actions should be such as to cause unnecessary ill feeling to anybody; he should not speak words which would unnecessarily cause ill feeling in the mind of another.

19. He should maintain those who are dependent on him: that obligation should be fulfilled. He should assign to them their proper work and should see that they do it right, or else they become harmful to him. If they get into vices etc., then he should assume such an attitude towards them that they may feel that he knows of their wrong doing. He should not ignore wrong doing or let the dependent persons get so vicious that their condition would lower his wisdom. Avoid a person if very bad: do not bring up serpents in your house.

20. Respect and render service to the Deva (i.e., the ideal, or Arhat), to the guest, and to poor deserving people. (The Deva has no commands – you take no commands from him).

21. With regard to eating and drinking. Eat and drink at the proper time in conformity with the nature of your constitution. But under all circumstances give up excessive eating because that particular food is liked by you.

22. When you feel that you are getting weak physically adopt the proper remedy for it.
23. Do not travel in countries which are full of criminals, or where there are other dangers, such as famine, plague, earthquake etc. The idea is self protection.
24. He should not act in such a way as to become unnecessarily hostile to the people; he should live in peace with them. (These rules are for the beginner and not for the strong in spiritual quality).
25. With reference to the attitude that he ought to have towards people that are ignorant, in a low state of development. The action should be such that they would feel that there is a higher life than their own. Let them feel the influence of the purer life of honesty, for instance.
26. He should avoid too much intimacy. Do not be too intimate with anybody.
27. Render service to those who have taken spiritual vows and who are experienced in the matter of wisdom and knowledge. Do some kind of service to them, and in that way you appreciate the wisdom and the vows, and in time the idea is to become like them. (This idea is not appreciated in the Western world: the philosophies of the West do not teach this idea). The idea here is that a man is a social being and must live in company of some sort, therefore he should establish certain relationships with the right kind of people in order by that means to become virtuous.
28. This is with regard to the several objects of life. There are four classes of life-objects, namely;

    (a) **dharma**, that is to say the practice of these rules – doing good;

(b) **artha**, which means the acquisition of the means of enjoyment, i.e. of wealth, property, etc.;

(c) **kāma**, which here has the broad meaning of 'desire'; desire for dress, for fame, for a nice house, for writing books – all desires;

(d) **moksha**, or liberation.

Seeing that the nature of karma is to obscure some quality of the soul, some idea of the nature of the soul in the state of liberation may be gained by remembering what particular quality of the soul comes out upon the removal of the eight classes of karma. This rule no. 28 is that the layman should accept (should have) all these four objects of life, but in such a way that a higher object is not sacrificed for the sake of a lower one; in such a way that there may not be any conflict between them. If there are difficulties in the way so far as kāma is concerned, then let it go but preserve dharma and artha. The order of these four objects is kāma, artha, dharma, moksha, the last being the highest.

29. In doing anything always consider your strength and your weakness; he should not undertake more than his strength will allow him to carry out.

30. Always attempt to rise higher and higher so far as the objects of life just mentioned are concerned.

31. Do or abstain from doing things that should be done or should not be done (respectively) at the right time. Stop doing a thing if it should not be done at that time.

32. The layman should hear the dharma every day. Or in the absence of a monk he should read or study it himself. The idea is that the practice of all these rules leads the man to the state of samyaktva. (So that having examined himself to see if the signs of samyaktva previously mentioned are in him and finding that he has

not attained the state of samyaktva, he will know now how to attain it; namely by putting these 35 rules of conduct into practice).

33. Avoid, or give up, obstinacy in all things. Obstinacy is here defined as the doing of an immoral, wrong or evil act with the object of hurting, injuring, or defeating another person. He should be yielding and not stubborn.
34. He should be partial for virtues; he should have all his energy directed for it.
35. With regard to opinions, beliefs, philosophies, religion, etc., he should be critical, and reconcile all the questions and solve all the doubts that arise out of this critical attitude.

That is the end of the rules which when practiced lead towards the reaching of the state of samyaktva, but the state is not actually reached until the three processes which were mentioned have been passed through. The result attained after passing through these processes is the Aupashamika samyaktva, or that state of samyaktva which is the result of the control of the three darshana mohaniya karmas and the four anantānubandhis.

The nature of the control here spoken of is such that these particular mohaniya karmas do not rise or become active. The man whose anantānubandhi anger is controlled does not get angry in that intense degree.

4th GUNA STHĀNA or Avirati-samyak-drishti-guna-sthāna

Drishti means attitude. It is a noun. Samyak is an adjective and means right or proper. Avirati means no control (here it means lack of control except of the anantānubandhis. No control of the sense pleasures and other karmas than the anantānubandhis of the mohaniya division). Guna means quality, and sthāna means stage.

All persons in this fourth guna-sthāna have control of the darshana and anantānubandhi mohaniya karmas (or kashāyas). Besides this factor, there is the other factor of samyaktva. So the characteristics of this fourth stage are;

(a) Lack of control, (of sense pleasures &c)

(b) Right attitude.

Kashāya means that which soils.

The lack of control here is also lack of control of the sense pleasures. Persons in this stage, while they do not have this self-control, still they do appreciate the value of self-control but through weakness they are not able to practice it. These living beings can be classed under three heads:

1. These (a) know the value of self-control; but (b) they do not make the effort to acquire it; and (c) they do not actually practice the things which constitute self-control. In illustration of this class of person the Indian Prince Shrenika was given.

2. These (a) know the value of self-control; (b) do not make the effort to acquire it; but (c) are actually doing the things which are done when self-control is possessed and practiced.

   There are certain devas and they are classed under 'avirati' because their practice of the things which constitute control is due merely to their circumstances and not to their own individual control of the desires. That is to say their non-indulgence is not due to self control. No human beings are in this second class. The faculty of control is not present (is not able to operate) when the living being is in a vaikriya or subtle body.

If a desire becomes active it is at once satisfied, the person does not have the power of self-control (it is of course potential or inoperative).

3. These (a) know the value of self-control, (b) make the effort to acquire it, but (c) are too weak and so they do not practice self-control. They make the effort but fail.

In this fourth stage of development there are 46 out of the 57 causes of karma already described, operative. Those which are inoperative are:

5 Kinds of mithyātva

4 Anantānubandhis

Āhāraka yoga

Āhāraka mishra yoga

making eleven inoperative causes (called 'hetu'. 'Hetu' is the means whereby, the instrumental cause).

The āhāraka body cannot be produced without perfect control of the sense pleasures &c.

In this 4th stage of development or guna-sthāna, the person is liable to generate any one of 77 out of the total 122 karmas. These 77 are as follows:

5 Jnānāvaraniya karmas,

6 Darshanāvaraniya karmas

2 Vedaniya karmas

19 Mohaniya karmas

2 Ayuh karmas (naraka and tiryancha omitted)

37 Nāma karmas

Out of 67, 30 being omitted, namely:

Naraka gati

Tiryancha gati

1, 2, 3, & 4, sense organs,

Āhāraka sharira

Āhāraka upānga

5 last bone joints (only the best bone joint is generated in this stage).

5 last kinds of samsthāna.

Naraka anupurvi

Tiryanch anupurvi

The bad gati karma (vihayo-gati)

Ātāpa (warm light)

Udyota (cool light or lustre)

Stāvara (stationary body)

Sukshma (minute body)

Aparyāptā (dies)

Sādhārana (common body)

Daurbhogya (unpopular)

Duhsvara (unmusical)

1 Gotra karma

5 Antaraya karmas

making 77 liable to be generated.

5th GUNA STHĀNA
or
Desha-virati-samyak-drishti-guna-sthāna

Desha means 'part' or partial; virati means control.

In all the guna sthānas above the third there is samyaktva and where there is samyaktva there is control of the darshana rnohaniya and of the four anantānubandhis; therefore the partial control here spoken of is of other kashāyas, sense pleasures, and karmas than these seven.

The factors of the person's state who is in this fifth stage are, therefore: (a) partial self-control and (b) samyaktva. The person in this stage is not able to practise complete self control. For instance, he can practise the principle of non-killing in only a partial way.

There is only one class of persons in this stage; they all know the value of self control, they all make the effort to practise it, and they practise it in part.

In this stage there are 39 out of the 57 causes operative. The following are the 18 inoperative causes:

5 Mithyātvas

4 Anantānubandhis

The apratyākhyāni (four of them, see below)
Avirati regarding moving living beings

The āhāraka yoga

The audārika mishra yoga

The āhāraka mishra

The kārmana yoga.

that makes 18 inoperative causes.

The apratyākhyāni are the anger, pride, deceitfulness and greed in the degree next above the anantānubandhis, and by reason of the presence or activity of them you are not able to take certain particular vows not to do certain things. And as in this desha-virati guna sthāna these apratyākhyāni are partially controlled, you can take the vows of refraining from certain activities.

The audārika mishra yoga means the activity of the physical body in the state of incompletion (aparyāptā) when completion is not going to lake place. It is only applied to living beings who die before birth.

The āhāraka mishra yoga would be any activity of the

āhāraka body when you were proceeding to make it, but are going to fail in completing it.

When in the kārmana sharira there cannot be any control. (There is no control in the deva or naraka states).

The karmas liable to be generated in this stage are:

5 Jnānāvaraniya karmas

6 Darshanāvaraniya karmas

2 Vedaniya karmas

15 Monaniya karmas

1 Ayuh karma (Deva)

32 Nāma karmas

1 Gotra karma

5 Antarāya karmas

making 67 liable to be generated out of 122.

These are the same as the 4th guna sthāna, only the following are not generated:

The apratyākhyāni, which makes four less of the mohaniya karmas; the manushyāyuh karma is not generated in this stage. Of the nāma karmas the following 5, as well as the 30 of the previous or 4th stage or guna sthāna, are not generated:

Manushya gati

Audārika sharira

Audārika upānga

Samhanana (vajra &c)

Manushyānupurvi.

Activity of the physical body does not necessarily generate the physical body.

When there is perfect self control there is no question of degrees of self control; but here in this 5th stage the person practises only a partial control over his sense pleasures, passions, emotions, desires, etc., and therefore the question arises as to what extent they practise such control.

In this partial control three degrees may be considered:

1. Lowest,
2. Middle,
3. Highest.

We will take each of these in their order in detail:

Lowest Degree of Partial Self-control

In the lowest degree of self-control in the samyaktva state the person would resolve and carry out the resolution, not to destroy any living being having the power of locomotion, intentionally when it is not guilty, and without any special necessary cause.

He would give up meat eating and liquor drinking.

He would every now and then try to concentrate upon the five great personalities postulated by the Jain philosophy.

Middle Degree of Partial Self-Control

1. In this middle degree of self-control the person may observe all the 35 rules of ordinary dharma previously given.
2. He performs six daily activities.
3. He observes the 12 rules of conduct, which may be called vows.
4. He would follow the path of rectitude; his conduct would be good.

Highest Degree of Partial Self control

1. He would give up all kinds of food which are animated at the time of eating (fruit, raw vegetables).

2. He would eat only once a day (a Jain eats only twice a day – or rather no Jain eats more than twice a day, some eat only once, and some not that).
3. He would practice absolute chastity.
4. He would *have the desire* to adopt the vows of the monk: he may not be able to adopt them, but still he has the desire to adopt them.
5. He retires from business. (This gives the younger men a chance to come in).

Six Daily Activities

Spoken of under the heading of the middle degree of self-control these are the daily activities:

1. He would worship the Arhat; or in the absence of the Arhat he would worship the image of the Arhat. This needs a little explanation in order that it may be understood. One might ask "What is the use of worshipping an image ?" The methods used in cognizing any insentient thing or living being are of four kinds, namely, name, sthāpanā (or âkriti), dravya, and bhāva. Nāma the first method, is by giving the name. The mention of the name is sufficient to bring to knowledge the idea of the object. The mention of names has a great deal to do with the rise and improvement of the consciousness; the mention of names is a great factor in those concrete activities which have to do with the progress of man.

   Sthāpanā, the second method by which we cognize things, pay respect to things, look down upon things, etc., is the picture, photograph, diagram, symbol, image, model, statue &c. It is also called ākriti, which means literally a drawing, image, or photograph. Absent persons can be worshipped by this means. The fact of the false use of images by the common people must not be taken as a reason for ignoring the philosophical truth that the image is an important factor when its use is rightly understood. Photographs &c., of absent friends can be used as a means of respecting them. Photographs &c., can be used as a means of insulting an absent person (Guy Fawkes, for example); and so also they can be used for respecting and worshipping absent persons.

Dravya, the third method, is when you wish to respect or cognize or worship a thing or person who had not yet come into existence; you worship the previous state of that thing or person. By paying respect to the present person or thing you can pay respect to the future being or thing. For instance the Indian prince Shrenika is believed to be the soul who is to be the first Arhat of the next cycle, could have been respected and worshipped by using Shrenika in that way.

Bhāva, the fourth method of knowing a thing or being or paying respect to them, is by using the actual thing or being or respecting the actual person.

So these are four ways of worshipping the Arhat. When anyone has an ideal, then he respects it; and the idea of the ideal is much strengthened by worshipping; worshipping the ideal by any of the above four methods strengthens the belief and convictions regarding that ideal. Of course, anything which a man looks down upon or ridicules is not his ideal: if he has an ideal he respects it.

2. The second daily thing that a person having the middle degree of self-control in the samyaktva state would do would be to render homage to the teacher (guru).

3. Third, he would study philosophy every day.

4. He would practise some form of self control every day.
5. He would practise some form of austerity (tapas) every day, both physical and internal. Controlling hunger would be a physical one, assuming a posture in concentration would also be a physical one. Concentration would be an internal one. Austerities are not the line of least resistance.
6. He would do some kind of charity; but not in the sense where the giver is superior to the receiver; both are equal. There must be no idea of superiority (I take it that the reason is because where there is any idea of superiority there is the presence of pride and pride is an intoxicating karma obscuring knowledge and right belief and right action).

VRATAS (व्रत)

Approximately translated by the English word vows. But an analysis of the vrata is given below so that there will be no ignorance of what the vrata is, its content.

In this stage of development (the 5th) which is now being described, there is only PARTIAL self-control, and the details already mentioned in the low, moderate, and high degrees of partial self-control are for the purpose of showing more definitely what the partial control is. And it is further shown by knowing the 12 vows which a person in this 5th stage of development may take. (It should be remembered that these stages of development are not chronological but logical).

The I2th Vratas or Vows

The word 'vrata' is derived from 'vri' which means to select, or to choose; therefore literally a vrata means a kind of choice. But in the technical or idiomatic sense in which the word is used in the connection now under consideration there is also the meaning of choosing a right course, and then there is the implied effort of will in willing to so choose.

Choice implies that the person has before him several ways of conduct, and that he picks out one from among them. As it is persons in the fifth stage of development that are now being spoken of, these persons are in the state of samyaktva (and not mithyatva), and this means that their selection will be a right and proper one (persons in the state of mithyatva will not choose the path of rectitude).

The choosing of a right course of conduct man go many ways necessitates the exercise of the judgment and discrimination. And doing this is not following the path of least resistance, so that the exercising of the judgment in selecting a right course of conduct as distinguished from living a life where no such choice is made implies an effort of the will force.

So this word vrata in its technical meaning here implies all these ideas, namely:

1. There is the actual selection of the conduct;
2. There is the exercise of the judging faculty in distinguishing right from bad courses;
3. There is the effort of the will (virya), or in psychological language there is conation.

There is no such thing as taking a vrata and not carrying it out. It is a very strict matter, requiring the exercise of much care in the undertaking to do.

This idea of the vrata as above described is peculiarly Jain; there is no promising on oath to a superior deity or person; it is not a command or a decree issued by a deity to his subjects or creatures. The breaking of the vows means degradation; in the Jain philosophy, if a person breaks his vows he is degraded (that is all; he is not damned for ever). But the Vedic idea of a vrata is very different, (how or in what way different was not given).

The 12 vratas which a lay person (not a monk) can take may be divided into three classes:

1. The first five are called lesser vratas (anuvratas), which means lesser as compared with the vratas of the monk.
2. The next three vratas are called guna vratas. Guna literally means virtues, but here it means that they give a kind of nourishment to the first five; they support and are helpful to the first five.
3. The last four are called Shikshā vratas, literally disciplinary. They are such that when you are practising them you are making a preparation for the monk life.

FIRST VRATA

First vrata is called in Sanskrit sthula-prānātipāta-viramāna vrata. Sthula means rough or gross as distinguished from strict or subtle. Prānātipāta means separating the prānas (life forces). Viramāna means giving up. So the name of this vow means choosing to refrain from some killing; to refrain from destroying life, but not in a literal or strict sense.

Now the next thing is to know what killing is; and then what particular kinds or forms of killing shall be refrained from.

What Killing is

Killing is the tearing asunder or separating of the pranas through negligent activities (the word negligent here has a particular technical meaning).

Negligent Activities

Negligent activities are activities which take place when a person is in a state in which care and caution cannot be used. When a person is in any of the five following states he acts without care or caution; he does not exercise care and caution:

1. **Mada**; pride, through which a person kills. It implies arrogance and is a state which ignores the rights of other living beings.
2. **Vishaya**; sense, pleasure which leads to killing.
3. **Kashāya**; the kashāyas anger, greed, deceit; etc., lead to killing in their intense degree where the reason is lost as in wrath and anger.
4. **Nidrā**; sleep. We cannot exercise care and caution when asleep and may kill a living thing if it gets in the bed. Mothers even kill their babies in this state.
5. **Vikathā**; undesirable conversation which leads to passion, lust and excitement of mind and then to killing. Duels, for instance; fights and vows.

These five kinds of activities are what is meant above by negligent activities.

Prāns

Different living beings have different numbers of prānas (life forces) are as follows:

Beings with only one organ of sense possess for prānas, namely:

1. Touch,
2. Respiration,
3. Forces of body,
4. Duration of life (āyuh).

Beings with have only these four forces of life are vegetables trees, water beings, air beings and fire beings.

Beings with two sense organs have six prānas, namely the above four and also:

5. Sense of taste,

6. Force of speech.

   They have the means or power of communicating among themselves, which can be called speech. Shell beings and protozoa.

   Beings with three sesnse organs have seven prānas, namely the above six and also:

7. Sense of smell.

   Ants, lice, bed bugs are instances of such beings.

   Beings with four senses have eight prānas, namely the above seven and also:

8. Sense of sight.

   Wasps, bees, scorpions are instances of such living beings.

   Beings with five senses are of two kinds, the first kind has no mind (manas, mind as meant in the Jain philosophy), and these beings have nine prānas, namely the above eight and also:

9. Sense of hearing.

   And the second kind have mind as meant in the Jain philosophy and they possess ten prānas, namely: the above nine and also:

10. Force of mind.

    Beings with all the five senses of touch, taste, smell, seeing and hearing, and force of body, force of speech, respiration and life duration (āyuh) are generated by the perspiration of some persons during sleep. These beings with five senses but having no mind are very minute.

We see by the above the order in which the senses are developed. A two sense living being, for instance, never has touch and smell, it is always touch and taste; and so on. The living beings which come under the second kind of five sense beings with mind are men, animals, birds, fish (of course these are only illustrations not exhaustive lists).

So that when we are in any state in which we do not use care and caution and in that state we tear asunder any of these prānas, then it is killing. The Sanskrit word for killing thus defined is "hinsā". Hinsā can be done in the naraka (hell) state; but after the separation the prānas come together again however, the pain of dread anxiety etc., is felt. In the naraka state there is pain all the time, and it may last a million years or 10 years or a billion years. Still it comes to an end. There is also hinsā in the deva state. In the deva state there is more pleasure than pain.

Now with regard to what extent this first vow causes us to refrain from killing, or how much and what kinds of killing the layman may take a vow to refrain from.

In order to steer clear of killing it is well to know the various ways in which killing is done; this can be learned by observation of the conduct of the people, but a few of the ways may here be mentioned:

1. Hunting, fishing etc.
2. Vivisection.
3. The taking of feathers, skins, etc. for dress.
4. Killing for food, meat, game, fish etc.
5. In war.
6. For private revenge.
7. For religious purposes (so-called), as in sacrifices.
8. Killing insects, such as flies, gnats, &c because you think they trouble you.
9. Capital punishment etc. etc.

For the sake of illustration the following analysis is made of the state of mind of a person who is hunting, for sport. There are three factors;

(a) in this state of mind there is no thought about the pain and harm the person hunting is inflicting on the innocent creature hunted;

(b) the person is entirely taken up with his own pleasure;

(c) he has no feeling for the pain and suffering of the animal.

So we have three factors, namely, thoughtlessness regarding the pain inflicted, selfishness, and heartlessness.

With regard to vivisection, it is done for the purpose of gaining certain physiological knowledge. But, first, we have no right to Jain knowledge at the expense of other living beings and, second, our lack of knowledge is due to a knowledge obscuring karma and if we will remove it we shall have the knowledge without injuring the living beings. In the Jain idea of morality relationships with all living beings are considered and not merely relationships with man.

Now from the point of view of how much killing a layman can avoid, living beings can be divided into:

1. Those having the power of locomotion,
2. Stationary; trees, etc. and the layman cannot take a vow to refrain from killing the stationary ones.

Now for the sake of comparing the protection to life afforded by a layman with that afforded by a monk, we may represent full protection by the number 16. Therefore in this first division (to speak roughly) the layman's protection to life would be only half that afforded by the monk.

Now taking the killing of moving living beings, how much can the layman avoid ? There is killing them:

1. With determined intention, where he thinks 'yes, I want to kill them, and I am killing them'.
2. Killing them in household and personal matters,

cooking, digging foundations, etc. The layman cannot undertake to refrain from the latter kind of killing, and so again the protection to life as compared with the monk is reduced to 4.

Another point is that the beings which are killed with determined intention may either be:

1. Innocent, or
2. Guilty so far as your interests are concerned, and the layman cannot say he will not kill the guilty ones. A lion is guilty if he attacks you, also so is a burglar. So again the protection to life is reduced to 2.

Disregarding the guilty living beings we must now consider which of the innocent ones he can refrain from killing. Men when they kill innocent living beings intentionally do so either:

1. Without a proper necessary cause, or
2. For a proper necessary purpose.

The layman cannot undertake to refrain from the intentional killing of innocent beings when there is a proper necessary cause for doing it. And so again the protection to life is reduced to 1. Therefore the protection which a layman can undertake to afford to life is, in comparison with that afforded by the monk, as 1 is to 16.

The layman, then, can undertake to refrain from killing innocent moving living beings intentionally when he has no proper necessary cause.

First Vow of the Layman

So the first vow of the layman is "I shall not kill a moving living being with determined intention" when it is innocent, without a proper necessary "cause or purpose".

Incidental

Virtues and vices are states of the individual and can never be transmitted or transferred from one person to another. Each person develops his own state of virtue, just as he does his own knowledge. You cannot impart virtue to another person, you cannot inherit virtue (in the sense of receiving it). You cannot inherit knowledge or impart knowledge. You can supply a person with the means (such as books or lectures) whereby he can develop his own knowledge.

Aticharas

Now we come to the things which are partial transgressions of this first vow.

A vow (vrata) is observed in two ways, which in the absence of appropriate English names, may be called the subjective way and the objective way, or the external and the internal way. In the aticharas it is the subjective or internal way that is broken, while in the external way the vow is not broken, and therefore it is called a partial transgression of the vow.

We are now considering persons in the 5th or desha-virati stage of development, and in all these vows the chief idea is partial self-control (desha virati). And because there is the other factor of samyaktva, there is also love (dayā) as a factor in all these vows. In the following things which are aticharas both these factors (self-control and love) are absent.

1. **Bandha**; means fastening with a rope or chain, and it can be either a human being or an animal. It can be done merely for cruelty, or it can be done for some other purpose. The person who has taken the first vow never fastens a being up for cruelty – if he did it would be breaking the vow. When it is done with some other object in view than mere cruelty or torture, then it can either be for a necessary purpose, or without a

necessary reason. If it is done without a necessary reason, then it is an atichāra; if it is done through anger, or greed, or in any state of mind that is thoughtless of the life of the being, then it is an atichāra or partial transgression of the vow.

As a matter of fact the philosophy teaches that persons who take these vows (vratins) and shrāvakas ought not to keep such animals as have to be tied up, but if obliged to tie animals up, it should be done in such a way that in case of fire they can easily be let loose, and at once; or if it is a child or human being, it should be tied so that he himself could undo it in case of fire. If the tying when done for a necessary cause is done with care and thought for the life of the beings, then it is not an atichāra. A shrāvaka is a man (or woman, of course) who hears the teaching of the monk; a shrāvaka is a hearer, not a teacher.

2. **Vadha**; is the name of the second atichāra. It means to strike with a whip, to hit, or to beat with a stick or cane. This can be done for necessary cause, or without a necessary cause. If done without a necessary cause then it is an atichāra of the vow. If it is done for any necessary reason and is done with due care and caution not to injure, then it is not an atichāra. But it is always better to intimidate than to strike or beat; and beating should never be done on a tender or delicate part of the body. Docking horses tails would come under this.

3. **Chhavichchheda**; means to cut, pierce, etc. (the ears, for instance).

   (a) When done without a necessary reason is an atichāra of the vow.

   (b) If done for a necessary reason (to cure a disease, for instance) it is not an atichāra.

4. **Atibhārāropan**; means to overload an animal or person. If greed is the reason of the overloading, or any cause but extreme case of necessity, then putting such loads on the animal or person is an atichāra. If loads are put on, the strength of the animal (or person) should be known and less should be put on than it can carry.
5. **Anna-pana-nirodha**; means withholding food and drink.

   (a) If done for a cruel object it is an anāchāra.

   (b) If done without a necessary cause, but still not for mere cruelty, then it is an atichāra (anāchāra means breaking the vow, atichāra means partial transgression).

   (c) If it is done for any necessary or proper cause, then the animal or person (or child) should not be starved or underfed. Then it is not an atichāra.

The above particular cases are given as illustrations of ways in which the first vow can be partially transgressed. There may be other ways; for instance, anyone who believes in mantras or thought-forms, would be breaking the vow or partially transgressing it if he used these to injure or so that injury came to the person or animal. Any line of conduct which results in killing.

These twelve vows of which this first is one, are all based on dayā (love, kindness, thoughtfulness for others), the same as were the thirty-five rules of ordinary dharma. These twelve vows are the special dharma as distinguished from the ordinary dharma.

Fruits

It is the opinion of the Jain philosophy that the results of the observance of this vrata (vow) are good health, strong body, strong constitution, etc. in the future or next following life. No separation from friends, relations, or parents. There would be happiness, the legitimate pleasures of life, comforts, long life; he will have a good name, handsome features, and a youth-time that would be enjoyable. The results of killing would be the opposite of these things, such as lameness, some incurable disease, separation from friends and relations, sorrow, short life, misery and after that an incarnation in the low state (naraka).

It is the Jain idea that kings, emperors, rulers, queens, etc., go to the naraka state after this life, as a general rule, of course there may be exceptions. The reason is that during their life they ignore the rights of others to such an extent.

Just incidentally mentioned here – it is the mohaniya karmas which cover up the heart. The heart is covered up by the mohaniya karmas.

SECOND VRATA

It is called in Sanskrit sthula-mrishāvāda-viramana vrata.

Vāda means telling; mrishā means falsehood.

The vow therefore means the resolution to refrain from telling gross falsehoods.

Sthula or gross falsehoods are those in which there is an evil intention and knowledge that the statement is false.

The following are illustrations of kinds of falsehoods:

1. **Kanyālika**; literally falsehoods relating to young girls, but it is chosen to represent human beings. So one kind of falsehood is falsehood told about another person or persons.
2. **Govālīka**; literally means falsehood relating to cows. It is used to represent any animals. Therefore another kind of falsehood is falsehood told about animals, (such as when trying to sell them).

3. **Bhumyālīka**; falsehoods relating to footless property, such as ground, or goods.
4. **Nyāsa-ninhava**; means denying that you have received it when money or other deposit has been left with you.
5. **Kūta-sākshyain**; means giving false evidence either in or out of court.

These five kinds are sthula or gross forms of falsehood, as distinguished from subtle falsehoods.

Four Classes of Falsehoods

1. The denial of a fact. To deny that a thing exists.
2. The affirmation of that which does not exist.
3. The thing may be one thing and you call it another. You may call a cow a horse.
4. A statement that is injurious to others; either to the person to whom it is made, or to other persons. Such as "Go and steal"; "Well, Mr. blind man, how do you do". To make a statement (even a true one) which is injurious is false or wrong when made without proper right cause. Also under this kind of falsehood can be classed false names "You silly goose".

Causes

Lies and falsehoods are spoken by reason of certain states of mind; certain states of mind are forces which impel to the speaking of falsehood. These states are:

1. Anger; when in anger you make false statements (they may be true, but injurious), and even may tell intentional lies when angry.
2. Pride.
3. Deceitfulness.

4. Greed.
5. False attachment.
6. False aversion – hatred.
7. Laughing and joking.
8. Fear. All nations that are under the control of other nations tell lies through fear. Any form of slavery induces lies.
9. False politeness.
10. Sorrow. We ignorantly blame others when we are in sorrow.

These causes may impel to the telling of such lies as are not possible to be avoided by the layman; it is only gross falsehoods that he undertakes to avoid.

So the second vow would be something like this: "I shall refrain from telling falsehoods about any person, animal, or thing, knowingly and with the intention of injuring someone;" or, stronger: "I shall not with predetermination tell a falsehood when I am conscious of the injury it will do"; or: "I shall not knowingly and intentionally make a false statement that will be injurious to others", or: "I shall refrain from telling gross lies."

Further, the vow may be taken in several ways; for instance, "l shall observe this vow only in speech and not mentally and bodily"; or " I shall observe it only bodily"; or it can be taken to avoid only mental falsehoods. (Writing lies would be an instance of bodily lies, there is no speech but there is bodily activity).

Incidentally – in psychological combinations the result is different from either constituent or factor.

The Aticharas

The following are illustrations of the ways of partially transgressing this vow:

1. **Sahasābhyākhyāna**; literally means a rash and false accusation. If you rashly call a man a thief when he is not.
2. **Mithyopadesha**; here means giving an improper order that is injurious or harmful to others. Literally it means false instruction. If it is made intentionally then it is an anāchāra, it must be rashly or carelessly made in order to be only an atichāra. If you ask a person to tell a lie doing so carelessly, then it is a partial transgression.
3. **Guhya bhāshana**; has two meanings (i) divulging a thing that is secret, (ii) backbiting or slandering. And these things must be done unintentionally through carelessness or rashness. If it is done for the Government intentionally, then it is anāchāra.
4. **Kuta lekha**; literally means making a false document, imitation of other people's writing. Any false document. If the vow is taken as regards the body and not merely "I shall not *speak* a lie", then making a false document is a breach of the vow, because you have *made* a false document, but it is only a breach when done intentionally and knowingly. If it is done rashly and you do not enquire into the matter then it is only atichāra.
5. **Vishvasta-mantra-bheda**; divulging the secrets of friends, wife, etc. This disclosure leads to the shame, perhaps, of the friend, and it is harmful to him; hence there is breach.

As already mentioned under vow No. 1, these vows are taken internally and externally, and if the action falls short of the external breach but does not fall short of the internal breach, then it is called a partial transgression or atichāra, because the internal part is transgressed. And in the foregoing illustrations the fact that the internal part is transgressed is to be seen in the fact of the rashness and injury that accompany the action; these vows are undertakings to exercise self-control and to refrain from injuring others and when there is rashness or carelessness and injury in an action then the vow is not fully carried out. And because there is both rashness (or carelessness) and injury to others the above mentioned illustrations are atichāras, even if the actual words spoken are true.

Fruits

The fruit that you reap by observing this vow is:

1. People trust you; it creates trustworthiness.
2. You accomplish your best objects; otherwise you try to do something and fail.
3. Your words become fruitful and do not go in vain. You are liked by the people.

And then there are results which come in the future life much the same as in the first vrata.

Mithyātva

Some further details about mithyātva.

There are four primary stages of mithyātva, namely:

1. **Pradesha-mithyātva**: those kārmic atoms which remain in the state of sattā (dormancy) assimilated with the soul. There are seven divisions of this, namely the:

   Mithyātva mohaniya karma

   Mishra mohaniya karma

   Samyaktva mohaniya karma

   Anantānubandhi krodha

   Anantānubandhi māna

   Anantānubandhi māya

   Anantānubandhi lobha

2. **Parināma-mithyātva**: is the mithyātva in some actual state of mind; the mind is actually in some state which you call mithyātva, so that the mind is modified by reason of this mithyātva. There are five kinds, namely those five which were given among the 55 causes of the generation of karma.

3. **Prarupanā-mithyātva**: is the speaking of the mithyātva or the teaching of it; you actually say something; your belief is expressed in words, either for yourself or for others. For instance, if you call true dharma false dharma; false dharma true dharma; or that the sacrifice of animals leads to the highest state.

4. **Pravarthana-mithyātva**: is when you act out your wrong belief; it is the action resulting from the three previous stages of mithyātva.

Q. "Who is going to decide which is the false and which is the true line of conduct ?"

A. Then you are sceptical, you doubt the ability of the soul to know ! Consciousness is the final ground.

And, of course, it is by removing the mohaniya karmas that our consciousness comes to be right consciousness and in harmony with the external universe.

THIRD VRATA

Sthula-adattādāna-viramana vrata: dāna means taking; datta means given; 'a' means not. Therefore the name of the vow means a resolution to refrain from gross forms of taking what is not given.

Theft

The idea in theft is taking other people's property without the consent of the owner. There is the gross form which is anything taken that is considered valuable, when it is not given by the owner. And there is the mild subtle kind (sukshma), when the thing taken is not considered by its owner, or generally, to have a value. If you take a thing of value it is a breach of the vow. The other is not the breach of the vow, but try to avoid it.

Fruits

The result of the observance of this vow is that you are trusted by all people, you are considered a good man; and in that way you prosper; and it develops strength of character.

As far as the future life is concerned there is the higher state and the deva state. If the vow is not taken or you soil it, then the result is untrustworthiness, you cannot carry out your ideas; and then also there is legal punishment, and then in the future state there is a miserable state in which you are all the time in dependence for your maintenance.

These 12 vratas are the special dharma of the layman, which was mentioned under the heading of dharma.

Atichāras

The following five things will illustrate what partial transgression of the vow consists of:

1. Accepting or buying stolen property; you did not actually steal it, but you have possession of it without the real owner's consent.
2. Giving orders to thieves. If a man is known by you to be a thief and you say to him "Why are you idle ?" "Go on with your business" it is the same thing as telling him to steal. And the manufacture or supplying of burglars' tools is an atichāra.
3. Using false weights and measures; you do not actually steal, but you get more money from the person than you ought to get.

4. Smuggling, you steal from the government. This would include supplying an enemy with goods in time of war (If you do not want war, get away from the nation and become a citizen of a peace loving people who do not go to war).
5. Counterfeiting or imitating. That is, selling things as one thing when they are really another. This would include the adulteration of foods etc.

FOURTH VRATA

Sex passion. Maithuna is the Sanskrit word and means the whole sex passion, from the slightest desire to the full act of sexual intercourse. By the full act is meant what is called in physiology 'penetration'. Maithuna can be divided into two kinds;

(i) sukshma or subtle – any little perturbation or excitation of the sex organs through the rise of the passion,

(ii) sthula, or gross, that is, intercourse with a woman either mentally, in words, or actually.

People express language which means intercourse; and mentally they have intercourse, especially in dreams.

The exercise of the passion is sometimes spoken of (in Dr. Nicholson's Zoology, for instance) as the act of procreation. This is not accurate naming really, because when exercised it is not exercised as an act of procreation; there is no such motive. This is shown by the fact that means are taken to prevent procreation; and again by the fact that the act is always performed in secret and is acknowledged with shame; and also because if the satisfying of the passion were done only for the production of offspring then the function would not be performed more than once a year by man.

Ten Points

1. In Dr. Nicholson's Zoology, it is stated that the act of exercising the sex passion is very weakening to the person, bodily, and mentally; that it is a very great strain upon the whole system, and is very exhausting, and is therefore injurious. In performing this act the person injures himself so much.
2. According to the Jain philosophy and other philosophies the creative fluid can be changed into a higher substance which can be used for spiritual purposes if you know how to change it. It gives in fact, a strong will. Preserving and changing the substance is called 'ojas'.
3. There is a special Jain teaching, which is not the teaching of any other philosophical system, that in every act of sexual intercourse 900,000 five-sense organed beings but without mentality (which have already been mentioned) of the shape of the human being but very minute, are generated and killed. This must be taken on faith in the Arhat's teaching but then the Arhat has those eighteen characteristics which have been given.
4. All the virtues are set aside just at the time of intercourse. It is an intoxicating karma (mohaniya karma) which obscures right belief and right action.
5. The person does away with reason at the time.
6. It is the opinion of the Jain philosophy that the plans, ideas, intentions, and schemes of a person who is full of excessive passion do not bear fruit (or if they do it is owing to the working of a karma). His mind is all the time on beautiful women; he cannot have self control and concentration of mind.

7. The success of the control of nature's finer forces that are not generally known depends upon chastity.
8. The success of mantras also depends entirely upon chastity. It is not the vibrations of sound only which give effectiveness to a mantra; your mental activity, your views; and your whole life all go to produce a compound vibration which can be sent to and felt by a being in the higher realms. The mental state is more important than the vibration of sound.
9. There are a number of worldly disadvantages from the excessive exercise of the sex passion you lose and squander your money if you go with many women, you lose sight of your better desires; you cannot perform good actions; you lose respect for your superiors; you lose faith in scriptures; you cannot go to the Deva state after death, etc. etc.
10. The science of breath teaches that in every activity you have to use the forces of the subtle (not the ordinary) breath. And in this science all forces are measured by the number of subtle breaths you spend. The force which one uses in the following activities is shown by the number of breaths expended, and is greatest in the sexual act, and least in spiritual concentration:

    If in spiritual concentration 4 breaths are spent, then in exercising good thoughts you spend 6 breaths; in sitting in silence 10; in speaking 12; in sleeping 16; in walking 22; in sexual intercourse 36. This is the Jain view – and it is the subtle and not the ordinary breaths.

The action of sexual reproduction, or more correctly called the action of satisfying the sex passion, is very injurious to the individual; injurious to his own soul, binding it with karma and rendering it impure, causing ignorance and consequent misery.

The sex passion having been defined as subtle and gross,

and some information given concerning it, the next thing is to know man's relation to the sex passion; and in view of the kind of thing which it is, namely an injurious thing, it should be controlled and avoided; so we now consider.

Brahmacharya

Which means the control of the sex passion; and as the control may be either entire or partial, we two divisions:

1. Entire giving up; 2. Partial giving up.

1. Entire giving up of the sex passion would be to refrain all the time from either of the following eighteen ways of indulging – with a being having a deva body; with a being having a physical (audārika) body, either mentally, in speech, or actually by satisfying the passion yourself, causing or helping others to do so, consenting to others doing so. That makes 18 ways (3 x 3 x 2 = 18). This is the chastity of the monk.
2. We are now dealing with the fourth of the 12 special rules of the layman who wishes to advance spiritually; the point reached is that because the sex passion is injurious to spiritual progress, therefore it should be avoided. The layman, however, is not able to avoid it entirely, and so the thing is to know what means he can take to avoid and control the sex passion as much as possible.

The 4th Vrata is called sva-dārā-santosha-para-dārā-viramana vrata, and is the means which the layman may adopt for this purpose. That which he undertakes to retrain from is the act known in physiology as 'penetration'; and he may vow either:

1. to give up such act with other people's wives whether they are married to the man or only kept,
2. to be satisfied with his own wife.

He may also undertake to try to think no sex passion and to speak no words which mean sex intercourse and to use care in the matter of dreams. Also if he chooses he may undertake to have no wife other than his present one (so that in case of her death he would not be disturbed with passion towards another woman). And he may undertake to observe absolute chastity in the day time. Also to try to observe the following nine rules given below.

The meaning of the vow as far as the words go is sva means own; dārā means wife; Santosha means being satisfied with. This is the first part of the vow. Para means others; dārā means wives; viramana means refraining from, vrata means a choice or undertaking. This is the second part of the vow.

If the person takes the first part, namely that he will be satisfied with his own wife, then he must not go with any other woman, whether human, deva, or female animal. If he only takes the second part he only undertakes to keep away from the wives of others; he does not then undertake to keep away from prostitutes, etc.

Nine Rules

Knowing, or being convinced of the usefulness of the restriction placed upon himself, he can help himself to keep the vow by paying attention to the following nine points. They may be called hedges, to keep oneself away from self injury in the direction of sex passion.

1. Try to live in a building where there are no female animals or neuter living beings; and live in such a way that you do not have physical contact all the time with a woman, because it excites the passion.
2. Try not to indulge in lustful stories or conversations or talks about woman.

3. The person who has taken the fourth vow should try to avoid sitting on a seat for at least an hour after it has been occupied by a woman, because the vibrations are left there and they excite the passion. Sitting on a seat or any place is meant.
4. He should not look with a lustful eye or in the spirit of lust on those parts of a woman's body which are factors in arousing the passion.
5. He should not remain in a room next to one in which a man and wife are in bed together if the wall is thin enough for him to hear or know or guess what is going on, because it will arouse thoughts of passion.
6. He should not bring to mind the sexual enjoyment he had with his wife in former days.
7. He should avoid taking foods which are exciting or intoxicating, or stimulating, especially things that are very oily, containing too much fat, because they produce passion.
8. Even non-exciting and non-stimulating foods should not be taken in excess; he should not gorge himself, because a too great quantity of food will produce passion.
9. He should not embellish his body.

All the foregoing remarks apply equally to woman, although they are worded for men.

Aticharas

1. For a person who has taken the second part of the vow to have intercourse with any girl or woman who is not the wife of somebody would be to soil the vow.
2. And so it would if such a person hires a woman for a time.

3. Dwelling upon the desire or intercourse or; gratifying the desire in any unnatural or any artificial way; these are partial transgressions; they are crimes against his own soul.
4. Giving away another person's daughter in marriage; or helping or causing another person to get married. This is transgressing because you are doing things which further the act or exercise of sex passion, which passion is the basis of marriage.
5. Intense desire for sexual intercourse. But this is from a different point of view from the third illustration. Here it means constantly looking at woman with that lustful eye. It would also include continuing in the act after it is over. And it would include a person who tries all sorts of medicines to make him strong if his sex passion is feeble.

FIFTH VRATA

Sthula-parigraha-parimāna vrata. Sthula means gross, parigraha means acquiring as one's own; that is possession. Parimāna means limitation. Therefore the vow means a choice to put a limit to the things you possess or will possess and in an ordinary way.

It is the limitation of the desire of possessing, and hence of actual possessing. A person may possess without desiring to possess.

To limit the desire is to partially control the desire; if the desire is uncontrolled it is limitless. To satisfy this desire for possession you have to be engaged in some kind of activity, and this activity is such that karmas are generated. Desire for things which are not yourself is here meant. A desire for knowledge is not meant. The real self is different from things, and is different from the body, and when this is *realised* it will be seen that the desire to possess, which is the false identification of the real self with material things, must be removed, and if this realisation is very strong the person will adopt full control; but if he cannot, do the full control he can *limit* his desires. Avirati (non-control) is the same thing as limitless desire. It means lack of control, and the desire is called ichchhā.

Fruits

The result of limiting the desire is contentment; discontent and happiness cannot go together. Non-limitation of desire is the same thing as unsteadiness; it is like the butterfly life. So long as there are these desires you have to wander from incarnation to incarnation. A desire for right knowledge is a desire for getting away from material things (from the possession of them). Knowledge is yourself; is the very nature of the soul.

Old method of classifying property into things:

1. Which can be sold by number, such as apples, melons.
2. Which can be sold by weight, such as sugar, drugs.
3. Which can be sold by measure, such as oil, milk.
4. Which can be sold by testing, such as gold, silver.
5. Different kinds of grades of property, such as land, buildings, metals, animals.

Atichāras

The atichāras of this vow are all based upon the above classification. You limit the quantity you will possess, as your own, and if you keep more than the specified quantity you break the vow; and subterfuges, etc., would be considered as partial transgressions. For instance, when you come to possess grain beyond the limit fixed by you, if you keep the excess part somewhere else, with somebody else, for a time that is subterfuge. Or marking a gold ring into a tie pin because your number of gold rings is reached, that is subterfuge.

These first five vratas are the minor vratas, previously mentioned. They are so in comparison with the more strict vows of the monk.

The next three are the guna vratas, they help and support the first five.

SIXTH VOW
GUNA VRATAS

Dig-parimāna vrata. Dig means direction. The vow means the choosing to determine the distance up to which and not beyond which you will go or send your men. The limitation of the area in which you will live, including all directions, or motion, up, down, etc.

In all activities of a layman there is destruction of life and therefore when he fixes his area he proclaims to all things beyond that area that he shall not injure them. This vow helps the first and also the other anuvratas.

If we will work out the knowledge obscuring karmas we can know of the things going on abroad without actually going there (compare the avadhi means of knowing in the early part of the karmas).

Atichāras

If we transgress the limits through forgetfulness, or by accident, or by subterfuge, it is atichāra; otherwise transgressing the limits is breaking the vow.

SEVENTH VRATA

Bhogopabhoga-parimāna vrata. Bhoga means that which can be enjoyed or used many times, and upabhoga that which can be enjoyed or used only once, such as cakes (food).

Things which can be used are of these two kinds, therefore

the vow is to limit the number of things coming under these two heads.

This helps the first five vows.

This vow includes the limitation of the activities you will engage in to get the things you use. So there are two divisions in this vow:

1. In regard to the things that you enjoy. If a layman can he should use only things which are inanimate. If he cannot then he will have to use things that are animate; but he must number them and limit them; he should give up flesh foods, also things (vegetables) in which there are infinite lives in the one body, such as carrots, turnips, potatoes (things that grow underground). But there is more to be said on this point.
2. In regard to the activities in which the layman should engage in order to obtain the things he uses; they should be faultless, sinless (but not sin in the Christian sense, sin here means sin against your own soul, obstructing its virtues). If he is unable to avoid sinless business then he should give up such trades as involve cruelty to animals.

Aticharas

Such business as the following fifteen should not be practised by those who have taken the seventh vow.

1. Making and selling charcoal.
2. Agriculture, horticulture or gardening.
3. Making and selling carts, etc., or driving vehicles belonging to Oneself.
4. Driving or plying other people's vehicles, either as a servant, or hired.
5. Blasting rocks, digging mines, ploughing, etc.

6. Ivory business, necessitating the killing of elephants.
7. Lac, or any similar substance. Inserts get caught in it.
8. Liquids, for the same reason.
9. Poison.
10. Fur, hair.
11. Milling or water-pumping; fish get killed in large quantities.
12. Castrating.
13. Burning or cutting green forests, fields, etc.
14. Drying lakes, ponds, or reservoirs; the fish are killed.
15. Bringing up women for immoral purposes or animals for any cruel purpose in order to make money.

Partial Transgressions

Eating food that contains animate beings, etc. (see Tattvārthādhigama Sūtra, chapter 7, verse 30. Cf. Yogasāstra, III, 97).

EIGHTH VOW
(Anarthadanda-viramana vrita)

The Sanskrit name of this vow consists of five words the first of which is a negative; the second means profit, benefit, motive, aim, object, necessary reason, purpose, etc., the third word in the name means evils or bad effects, and the last two words mean undertaking to refrain from.

So this eighth vow is an undertaking not to incur unnecessary evils.

We bring unnecessary evils upon ourselves to no purpose, by indulging in thoughts, words, and deeds in which there is no benefit to society, to our friends, or to ourselves.

A layman cannot avoid the evils entailed by his necessary

pursuits; but he can undertake to avoid the evils entailed by unnecessary pursuits and activities such as thinking about, speaking about, or otherwise busying himself with matters that do not concern him or in which there is no benefit.

The following are some of the ways in which we do things in which there is no benefit:

> Constantly fearing the loss of any of the good things we have, – wealth, friends, health.
>
> Constantly fearing that bad things which we are at present without, may come upon us, pain, poverty, disease.
>
> Undue anxiety to get rid of disease, poverty, etc., when once they are upon us.
>
> Undue anxiety for the future craving for the enjoyment of happiness expected to come in the future.
>
> Being glad at having killed something or somebody, or approving of others who have done so.
>
> Speaking ill of or misrepresenting others, and boasting about it.
>
> Desiring the death of someone in order to inherit his or her property, or cheating people and boasting about it.
>
> Distrusting or wishing the death of others for the sake of the safety of our own property.
>
> Giving gratuitous advice about matters that are no concern of ours.
>
> Lending dangerous weapons gratuitously, like guns; or implements which in their use destroy life; – fishing tackle, garden tools.

Sheer carelessness of thought, word, and action such as drinking; excessive sensuous indulgence; things done, said, or thought through extreme anger, pride, deceitfulness, or greed;

excessive sleep; and also talk about matters which do not concern us, such as wars between other countries; talk about woman's bodily charms; about good dinners; and about kings.

By taking this eighth vow we use a means of guarding ourselves against many evils which we might otherwise incur to no purpose.

Transgression*

1. Gestures that arouse the sex-passion (Kandarpa).
2. Antics, tomfoolery (Kautkuchya).
3. Obtaining and keeping things that are not necessary for our worldly welfare (Bhogopabhoga Atireka).
4. Over talkativeness (Maukharya).
5. Leaving dangerous instruments ready for self-use more than are necessary, for lending the use of such instruments to others etc., etc, Samyukta adhikarana).

NINTH VOW
(Sāmāyika)

This is the first of the disciplinary vows (Sikshā-vrita). It is a vow by observing which one gets equanimity. It consists in thinking about the permanent self; or in reading true philosophy or scriptures; or in lamenting the wrongs one has done and strengthening the resolution not to repeat the wrong in future. Also revering the Master by recounting his merits. The time taken should be forty-eight consecutive minutes, predetermined and the vow should be taken to practise it a definite number of times a year, 12 times, 52 times, once a day, or some definite time.

---

* Tattvārth, S. VII, 27. Yogaśāstra III, 114.

The general idea of this vow is to sit in a certain place and read or meditate on holy subjects.

Partial Transgressions*

Misdirection of mind, speech, or body during the time of meditation. That is, the mind, the speech, or the body must not occupy itself with other subjects than the one in hand.

Practising the vow in a wrong place, that is where there are insects that you might kill while sitting or standing.

Forgetting the rites: i.e., leaving off in say 40 minutes when you have determined upon 48 minutes.

TENTH VOW
(Disavksika vrita)

Is reducing to a minimum the space in which we will move. It is undertaking to limit oneself to the space of one house, or one room for a day once a year at least. It is the sixth vow in a more restricted form; in one form it is daily to restrict our movements according to our needs. One should not do anything which is beyond the limit specified.

Partial Transgressions †

Ordering things beyond the limit. Sending some one on some business beyond the limit. Making some sound to attract the attention or some one beyond the limit.

Making some sign to some one beyond the limit to come to you. Throwing something to a person beyond the limit in order to attract his attention.

---

* Tattvārth, S. VII, 28. Yogaśāstra III, 115.

† Tattvārth, S. VII, 26. Yogaśāstra III, 116.

ELEVENTH VOW
(Pushdhopāvasa vrita)

The eleventh vow is the same as the ninth but continued for twelve or twenty-four hours and accompanied by some fasting. By fasting we remove impurities. If the vow is taken it must be practised at least once a year. If food is taken at all on the day of fasting, it should not be between sunset and the following sunrise. It is usual to keep to one place, do no business, and drink nothing or eat nothing for twelve, twenty-four, thirty-six, forty-eight or seventy-two consecutive hours once a week, once a month, or at least once a year.

Partial Transgressions*

1. The first of these refers more to India or any hot country; it is not being particular to avoid killing insects by one's clothes or one's bedding.
2. Not taking something to clear away whatever insects there may be.
3. Not being particular to avoid killing anything in performing the offices of nature.
4. Despising the ceremony itself.
5. Forgetting any of the necessary things to be done in this vow.

TWELFTH VOW
(Atithisaṃvibhāga vrita)

"Atithisaṃvibhāga" vow. Atithi means a guest, and saṃvibhāga means to distribute, share with. The vow is an undertaking to invite some Jain monk (or in the absence of a monk some respectable Jain layman, or in the absence of both,

*Tattvārth, S. VII, 29. Yogaśāstra III, 117.

to do so in thought), on the day following the fast undertaken in the previous vow, or whenever opportunity offers to partake of some of the food about to be eaten, without informing the guest of the vow to do this; and only the things which are partaken of by the monk should be eaten at the time. It is things which are necessary for life that are partaken of; and books, clothing, medicines etc., as well as food, may be offered to the person invited.

This vow, if taken, must be practised at least once a year.

Partial Transgression*

Offering food with life in it to a monk; fruit, for instance, not cut. After fifty minutes of being cut, fruit is considered to contain no life constituting the body of the fruit.

Putting living things among food which is free from life; for instance putting fresh cold water, which has life, with water that has been boiled. In the Jain belief fresh cold water is a mass of living substance, and not merely the home of minute life or animaculate.

Giving the food etc., in a grudging spirit.

Saying that something which the monk may have asked us for and which we do not wish to give belongs to a friend or some one else.

Inviting the monk at a time which we know to be after he has taken his meal.

That is the end of twelve special rules for helping to change ourselves from what we actually are, ignorant, mistaken, weak, injurious beings to what we potentially are according to the teachings of those Masters who have developed their spiritual qualities to perfection and have attained omniscience in the flesh.

*Tattvārth, S. VII, 31. Yogaśāstra III, 118.

The rules are based upon a certain foundation or character already developed, kindness of heart, self-control, desire for right knowledge, and relish of truth, the internal attitude accompanying the external, visible practice of the rules. These rules bring out further knowledge, increased strength of character, greater peace of mind, sympathy, and kindness, and lead to higher levels on the way towards an everlasting, blissful omniscience in a state of life which is natural to the real pure self, and which is open to all who wish to attain it.